skills

passing STANDARD GRADE HISTORY

Graeme Coy

Hodder & Stoughton

A MEMBER OF THE HODDER HEADLINE GROUP

Acknowledgements

The publishers would like to thank the following for their permission to reproduce copyright illustrations and photographs:

Camera Press (p. 37); Imperial War Museum (p. 66); David King (p. 38); Mary Evans Picture Library (p. 64); The Photomas Index (p. 63); Punch (p. 69); Topham Picturepoint (p. 68); West Dunbartonshire Libraries and Museums Service (p. 21).
Every effort has been made to trace and acknowledge ownership of copyright. The publisher will be glad to make suitable arrangements with any copyright holders whom it has not been possible to contact.

Orders: please contact Bookpoint Ltd, 39 Milton Park, Abingdon, Oxon OX14 4TD. Telephone: (44) 01235 400414, Fax: (44) 01235 400454. Lines are open from 9.00–6.00, Monday to Saturday, with a 24 hour message answering service. Email address: orders@bookpoint.co.uk

A catalogue record for this title is available from The British Library

ISBN 0 340 75342 0

Published by Hodder & Stoughton Educational Scotland
First published 1999
Impression number   10 9 8 7 6 5 4 3 2 1
Year   2005 2004 2003 2002 2001 2000 1999

Copyright © 1999 Graeme Coy

Typeset by Fakenham Photosetting Limited, Fakenham, Norfolk NR21 8NL
Printed in Great Britain for Hodder & Stoughton Educational, a division of Hodder Headline Plc, 338 Euston Road, London NW1 3BH by Scotprint Ltd, Musselburgh, Scotland.

Contents

Preface

This book is meant to help all candidates to do as well as they can in the History Examination at Standard Grade, and perhaps add to the understanding that students and their teachers have of what is expected in that exam. It is designed to support work done during the two years of the course, as well as to offer some suggestions for revision before the day of the examination.

The book covers each context in Unit I and the most popular contexts in each of the other two Units, relating to the requirements for examination in 1999 and after. The types of question shown and the answers suggested to them should provide valuable guidance for all contexts. The answers given should not be treated as models to be memorised, but rather as guides to what kind of approaches should be used and what type of evidence should be offered. Similarly, the time lines and glossaries are intended as frameworks to help revision or to be built on, rather than lists of facts to be memorised.

Graeme Coy, 1999

Introduction to this book and the examination

About this book

For many of you, Standard Grade examinations will be the first examinations set by people who do not actually teach you – in this case the Scottish Qualifications Authority. This book is written to help you if you are preparing to sit the Standard Grade examination in History. It will give you information about:

- the examination itself;
- how you can get the best grade at whatever level of the examination you sit.

Most of you will sit the examination at two levels:-

Foundation and General or General and Credit

This means you will find useful information and suggestions in almost every part of the book. Parts which deal with particular levels – Foundation, General or Credit – are clearly marked in the following way F/G/C so that you know what you should pay special attention to and what you can safely ignore. This book is meant to support the work you do in school over the two years during which you prepare for the Standard Grade examination. So here is the first piece of advice for you.

REMEMBER: Do work steadily over the two years and do not leave all your preparations for the examination till a week or two before you sit it!

Remember that your history course is split into **THREE** units.
- Unit I has three parts called 'contexts' and you will have studied only ONE of these.
- Unit II also has three contexts and you will have studied only ONE of these.
- Unit III has four contexts and you will have studied only ONE of these.

There is a lot to learn – far too much to do if you leave it all to the last minute!

Your course and the Standard Grade examination

During the two years you spend studying history before you sit the examination you will not only learn a lot of history but you will also come to know much more about how to study historical evidence and how to write about history.

This is why in the examination you sit, there are some questions which ask you to write about what you know – these are **Knowledge and Understanding questions.** You will find more help with Knowledge and Understanding Skills in Section 3 of this book. There are also questions which ask you about finding out from historical evidence – these are **Enquiry Skills questions.** You will find more help with Enquiry Skills in Section 2 of this book.

Foundation level

At this level you actually write on the examination paper and there will be sources to help you. You will be able to see what type each question is on the paper:
- by looking on the right hand side of each page to see whether the mark for the question is in the KU or ES column;
- by seeing that, in Unit I contexts, some questions are put under a heading which shows they are about Investigating a topic in history.

Investigating is another way of saying 'finding out' and is all about Enquiry Skills.

General level

At this level you will find that every context in the examination paper is in two parts.
- **SECTION A** is called **KNOWLEDGE and UNDERSTANDING.**
- **SECTION B** is called **ENQUIRY SKILLS.**

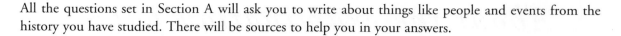

All the questions set in Section A will ask you to write about things like people and events from the history you have studied. There will be sources to help you in your answers.

> **REMEMBER: To get full marks for any question in Section A you must add at least ONE relevant fact from your memory to what you find in the sources**

Every context in Section B is called Enquiry Skills. In Unit I contexts the Enquiry Skills are all about investigating an issue in history. An issue is something about which it is possible to have more than one opinion. You will have to use the Enquiry Skills you have learned, to study the sources you are given and then to give your own conclusion, that is – what you think about the issue.

This means that in each Unit I context the last question will ask you what you think about the issue you are investigating. To gain full marks for this question you will be need to use information from the sources you are given **and** at least one piece of evidence about the issue which comes from your own memory.

In the contexts in Unit II and Unit III, the questions ask you to write about the sources you are given as historical evidence. For example – *Is Source D valuable as evidence about . . .?* One question in these contexts may ask you to use something you remember as part of your answer, to gain full marks. If you need to use your own knowledge you will find this clearly shown in the question itself.

Credit level

At this level you will find that every context in the examination paper is in two sections.
- **SECTION A** is called **KNOWLEDGE and UNDERSTANDING**.
- **SECTION B** is called **ENQUIRY SKILLS**.

There are no sources for you to use in Section A, but there are short quotations before each question. Read these carefully because they will start you thinking about what the question is asking you to do. ONE question in either Section A or Section B will ask you to write a short essay of several paragraphs. This type of question will have 8 marks and will give you a choice of a) or b). Make sure you look out for this question.

Section B in every context is called Enquiry Skills. In the contexts in Unit I, the Enquiry Skills section is about investigating an issue in history – that is, something about which it is possible to have more than one opinion. You will have to use the Enquiry Skills you have learned to study evidence in sources and then give your own conclusion on the issue – that is, say what you think about it.

In contexts from Unit II and Unit III, the questions ask you to write about sources as historical evidence. For example – *Do Sources A and B agree about . . .?*

One question in these contexts may ask you to use something you remember as part of your answer, to gain full marks. If you need to use your own knowledge you will find this clearly shown in the question itself.

About the examination papers themselves

Many of you will have seen past papers and will know what to expect when you sit down to take the actual examination. But what you will have worked with before may have been only part of the whole examination paper, with the contexts you have studied in it. At each level the final examination paper will have ALL the contexts in each of the units.

Almost everyone will be a little nervous before the examination begins. This can help to make you feel alert and actually make you work well, but nerves can also make you misread or overlook things in an examination.

REMEMBER: To make sure you avoid mistakes in what you do in the examination, look at the cover of the examination booklet very carefully. Then . . .

Foundation level

You write on the examination booklet itself. The cover of your examination booklet will ask you to fill in things like your name, school, date of birth and candidate number. The next page tells you what the booklet contains.

Find those parts – contexts – you have studied and your teacher has told you to look for and mark them on the booklet. Look at the example provided to help you.

FOR OFFICIAL USE					
Presenting Centre No.	Subject No. 1540	Level	Paper No.	Group No.	Marker's No.

F

(KU)　(E)

Total Mark

1540/101

SCOTTISH CERTIFICATE OF EDUCATION　9.30 AM – 10.30 AM

HISTORY STANDARD GRADE Foundation Level

Fill in these boxes and read what is printed below.

Full name of school or college

Town

First name and initials

Surname

Date of birth
Day　Month　Year　Candidate number

Number of seat

Turn to **page three** when you are told to do so.

Before leaving the examination room you must give this book to the invigilator. If you do not, you may lose all the marks for this paper.

You must do ONE context from Unit I and ONE context from Unit II

UNIT I – CHANGING LIFE IN SCOTLAND AND BRITAIN

Choose only ONE Context. This should be the Context you have studied.

Context A: 1750s-1850s...........................Pages 4-7

OR

✓ Context B: 1850s-1950s...........................Pages 8-11

OR

Context C: 1880s-Present Day...................Pages 12-15

AND

UNIT II – INTERNATIONAL COOPERATION AND CONFLICT

Choose only ONE Context. This should be the Context you have studied.

Context A: 1790s-1820s...........................Pages 16-20

OR

✓ Context B: 1890s-1920s...........................Pages 21-25

OR

Context C: 1930s-1960s...................Pages 26-30

Write your answers in the spaces provided.

Some sources have been adapted or translated.

[Turn over

Page three

If you do this carefully then you will not:
- do more contexts than you need to
- attempt contexts you have not studied.

> **REMEMBER: At Foundation level you will be answering questions on:**
> - **ONE context from Unit I**
> - **ONE context from Unit II OR Unit III. (You will know which Unit before the examination and only one will be in the examination booklet.)**

G General level

You write your answers in a separate answer book and need to fill in things like your name, school, date of birth and candidate number on this.

The cover of the examination booklet tells you what the booklet contains and on what pages.

> **REMEMBER: You must attempt THREE contexts only, ONE from each of the three units. Look on the cover of the examination booklet in each unit for the contexts you have studied and mark them clearly – as shown in the example below.**

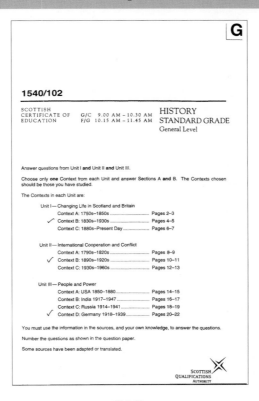

If you do this carefully then you will not:
- do more contexts than you need to
- attempt contexts you have not studied.

Credit level

You write your answers in a separate answer book and need to fill in things like your name, school, date of birth and candidate number on this.

The cover of the examination booklet tells you what the booklet contains and on what pages.

REMEMBER: You must attempt THREE contexts only, ONE from each of the three units. Look on the cover of the examination booklet in each unit for the contexts you have studied and mark them clearly – as shown in the example below.

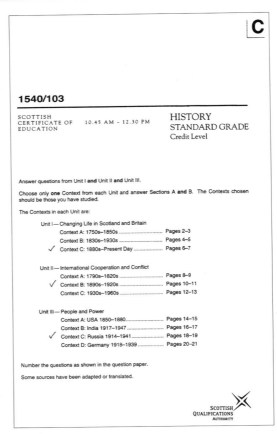

If you do this carefully then you will not:
- do more contexts than you need to
- attempt contexts you have not studied.

Foundation/General/Credit

The examination is your chance to show what you have learned during your history course. The examiners are trying to help you to do this by asking questions about things you are likely to know from your studies. Read the questions carefully because they will help to show you how to answer. For example, if the examiners want you to make a judgment about something or someone, the question will often look like this:-

Why was the assassination of Archduke Franz Ferdinand in 1914 so important?

Look at the number of marks given to each question. The number will give you an idea of how much evidence you need to use to obtain full marks for the question. As a rough guide you should think of one relevant fact for each mark.

Sections 2 and 3 of this book will give you more help on how best to answer the different types of questions you will find in the examination papers.

Preparing for the examination

Much of the work you do during the two years of the Standard Grade history course is preparation for the final examination. You will gradually gain the knowledge and skills you need to succeed in the examination. It is important to work steadily during your course so that:

- you become very sure of what you know, by going over it several times
- you become confident about the skills you need by practising them many times.

The time you have to read and write when you sit the examination is not long, so it is important to:

- make sure you know what the examination papers will look like;
- be sure which contexts you are ready to use;
- practise working with source evidence.

General and Credit

As well as notes you have from the two years of your course you may find revision is helped by the use of summaries of major facts from the contexts you have studied. You can make these for yourself and this is a good way to help you remember information. You should also:

- practice identifying the kind of answers questions expect you to write;
- practice investigating using several sources which disagree about an issue and then giving your conclusion.

C Credit

Practice writing essays with several paragraphs:-
- describing events, situations or people;
- explaining why something happened or what its results were;
- saying why something was important.

Working steadily through the two years of your course will make revision just before the examination much easier and more successful.

Whether you are sitting the examination at Foundation, General or Credit levels you should avoid working late on the night before the examination. You will be more successful if you are well-rested and alert on the day of the examination.
- Your answers will be better.
- You will be much less likely to make mistakes, such as attempting the wrong context or missing out questions.

REMEMBER: At Foundation and General levels the evidence you need to pass will be in the examination paper you see on the day of the examination. What you must be able to do is to use it correctly.

Enquiry Skills

Introduction

This chapter is split into separate Foundation, General and Credit parts, to make it easier to use. Most of you will find help in two of the three, depending on whether you are preparing to sit the examination at Foundation and General levels or General and Credit levels.

Each part is organised in the same way:

- a short introduction to remind you what you are revising;
- an example of each of the skills;
- questions for you to attempt.

REMEMBER: At ALL levels Enquiry Skills are the more important part of the examination, carrying more marks than Knowledge and Understanding questions.

 ## Foundation/General/Credit

At Foundation, General and Credit levels ALL Enquiry Skills questions will have sources for you to use. In most of the questions, all the evidence you need to get full marks is in the sources on which they are based. You should have the skills to use the evidence.

General/Credit

At General and Credit levels, and in a very small number of questions, you will also need to use some of your own evidence as well – to obtain full marks.

Where you need to use information from your own memory in a question – this will be clearly shown in the question itself.

> REMEMBER: Whatever levels you attempt, always read the introduction to each source, the source itself and the question(s) which follow very carefully.

You will find answers to all questions given for you to try at the end of Section 2.

Foundation level

By the time you sit the final examination you will have learned at least FIVE important Enquiry Skills. You will be able to:–

1 give reasons why a source is or is not useful, valuable or reliable, depending on what the question says;
2 give the point of view shown by a source;
3 compare the evidence in two sources;
4 find and record relevant evidence from two or more sources;
5 write down what you have found out about a topic from two or more sources.

> REMEMBER: In all of these five cases, the evidence you need to answer any questions is in the sources in the examination paper and the information you are given about them.

An example of each of these five skills is given below and is followed by some questions for you to try.

> REMEMBER: You will always know an Enquiry Skills question because the marks for it will be under ES in one of the two columns on the right side of the page in the examination booklet.

1 Looking at the value, usefulness or reliability of a source

In this case you will be told that a source is useful, valuable or reliable, or possibly that it is a good source. You will be expected to find reasons for saying this from the evidence in the source. Here is an example:
A few years before the start of the First World War the German Emperor said this about England.

Source A

It is an insult if England will only be our friend if we keep our navy small. If England wants war, we shall give them what they are asking for.

*Why is Source A useful as evidence about relations between Germany and Britain before the First World War? Give **three** reasons.*

Reason ....
....

Reason ....
....

Reason ....
....

The question says that the evidence in Source A is useful, so you are looking for three reasons to show that it is.

> **REMEMBER: Source evidence is useful if:–**
> * the source comes from very close to the time of the event, it is about – that is, it is a primary source;
> * the author of the source is directly involved in the event, or is an eyewitness to it, or is someone important who would know about it;
> * the source gives clear and relevant evidence about the event;
> * the source gives a lot of relevant evidence about the event.

In this case, **three** things from the list above can be used.

First look back to what you are told about the source. You are told two things:

1 that it comes from a few years before the First World War – which makes it a primary source;
2 that its author was the German Emperor himself – an important man in relations between Germany and Britain.

Now read the source again. It is short, but clearly shows relations between Germany and Britain were not good.

Your answer should look like this:

Reason *It is a primary source OR It comes from just before the First world War.*
Reason *It is by the German Emperor himself.*
Reason *It tells you Germany and England were arguing.*

All the evidence you need has come from the source and its introduction.

> **REMEMBER: Do not copy out the whole source introduction. You will waste time and simply copying does not get you marks.**
> **Do not write out everything the German Emperor says about Germany and England not getting on well, because you will only gain one mark for repeating content from a source, no matter how much of it you write!**

Now here is an example to try for yourself:
In Source B Captain Gilbert Nobbs described the effect of machine gun fire in July 1916.

Source B
The front line jumped from the trench and walked into the open. Machine guns sprayed their deadly fire backwards and forwards. In far less time than it takes to write it, all the men in the front line all seemed to vanish.

1   Why is Source B useful evidence about the effect of machine guns during the First World War? Give three reasons.

Reason ....
....
Reason ....
....
Reason ....
....

2   *Giving the point of view of a source*

In this case you will be expected to find out what the author of a source thinks. Or you may be told what the author thinks and asked to show how we know this. Here is an example:
In 1917 the Tsarina wrote to her husband, the Tsar, about the possibility of revolution. Source C is part of her letter.

Source C
This is just a hooligan movement. Young people run about and shout that there is no bread, simply to create excitement. If the weather was very cold they would probably all stay at home. All this will pass and become calm.

What does Source C show you about the Tsarina's views on the threat of revolution in Russia? Mention two things.

She thought ....
....
She thought ....
....

This question is asking you to find out the Tsarina's views on revolution.
In this case the introduction to the source helps you understand what it is going to be about, but gives you nothing else to use. All the evidence you need is in the source itself.

You are asked to give the Tsarina's views on revolution and must use two pieces of evidence to get full marks. She actually tells you four things that she thinks:

- that it is hooligans who are involved;
- that it is young people who are rushing around just for excitement;
- that if the weather were bad it would not be happening;
- that it will all be over soon.

So your answer could be this.

She thought that it was just young people looking for fun.

She thought that it would be over soon.

REMEMBER: You are asked to say what she thought according to the source NOT if she was right about the danger of revolution. You should not give any of your own knowledge in this question. Nor will you get a mark for saying that it is a primary source.

Now here is another example for you to try:

In Source D a modern historian explains why the Bolsheviks gained power in Russia.

Source D

The Bolsheviks had many enemies but their enemies were weak, divided and slow to act. Lenin's plan was to make them even more divided and take advantage of their slowness to act.

2   *What does the writer of Source D think of the enemies of the Bolsheviks? Mention* **two** *things.*

He thinks ....

....

He thinks ....

....

3   Compare the evidence of two sources

In this type of question there will be two sources to look at and then you will find a question which asks you to compare the evidence in both of them. Usually both sources will be written but one may be a picture or a table of figures. Here is an example:

The next two sources are about making a first train journey.

Source E was written in 1830.

Source E

I can't call it a pleasure, taking a trip of five miles at twenty miles an hour. It really is flying. It is impossible to forget that any little accident means instant death. It gave me a headache which has not left me yet.

Source F was written in 1837.

Source F

I soon felt quite secure and the speed was delightful. All other ways of travelling are irritating and boring by comparison.

*Read Sources E and F carefully. Give **two** ways they disagree about train travel.*

In this type of question you are told the sources do not agree about something – train travel. You have to find two examples of this disagreement. This means you will need **four** pieces of evidence in total. Your answer should look like this:

Source E says the journey was not a pleasure but Source F says it was delightful.
The writer of Source E is afraid he will be killed but the writer of Source F feels quite safe.

REMEMBER: All the evidence you need is in the two sources – but you must make full use of both of them. Make sure that you complete your comparison by writing out what each source says about the train journey. DO NOT write your answer in this way:

Source E says the journey was not a pleasure and Source F disagrees.
The writer of Source E was afraid and the writer of Source F disagrees.

If you write your answer like that you will only get 1 mark.

Now here is a question for you to try:

These two sources are about the Youth Movement set up by Hitler.
In Source G a girl describes the Youth Movement.

Source G

We had to be present at the rallies and sports. Weekends were full of outings, campings and marches. It was all fun in a way and we got plenty of exercise.

Source H is also about the Youth Movement, but was written by a different girl.

Source H

I felt bored. We were expected to worship a flag as if it was God. We had to stand for hours and listen to boring speeches.

*3   In what **two** ways do Sources G and H disagree about the Youth Movement set up by Hitler?*

Source G says . . . .
But Source H says . . . .
Source G says . . . .
But Source H says . . . .

Enquiry Skills 4 and 5 are part of **Investigating** and you will only be asked questions needing these skills in Unit I contexts. You will find the final questions in the Unit I context you are attempting are separated from the rest of the question in the context by the words:
In Questions 4, 5 and 6 the topic for investigating is . . .

Here is an example of an investigation to help you see what you need to do:
In Questions 4, 5 and 6 the topic for investigating is: Working conditions in cotton mills before 1850 Study the information in the sources, and then answer the questions which follow.

Source I is from evidence given in 1830 by a young cotton mill worker in Paisley.

Source I
There is a great deal of dust and it makes me hoarse and I cough. I am sometimes short of breath. I have pains in my ankles at night from the long standing at work.

4   *Why is Source I good evidence about work in a cotton factory? Give two reasons.*   2 marks

Because . . . .
       . . . .
Because . . . .
       . . . .

Source J is part of a description of a cotton mill. It was written in 1833.

Source J
Gilchrist's mill at Inverbervie is dirty, low–roofed and badly ventilated. There is no attempt made to remove dust. Machinery is not boxed in and the spaces in between are so narrow they can hardly be seen.

Source K is a description of another cotton mill. It was also written in 1833.

Source K
The windows of the mill open from the top and the rooms are well ventilated. There is no unpleasant smell anywhere and everything is clean and neat. Dust is thoroughly removed.

5   *What does Source J tell us about working conditions in a cotton mill?*
     What does Source K tell us about working conditions in a cotton mill?   4 marks
6   *Write down your findings about working conditions in cotton mills before 1850.*   2 marks

Answers
4   *Because it is a primary source.*
     Because it comes from someone who actually worked in a cotton mill.

(This is just a question about the value of evidence and is the same as Enquiry Skill number 1)

5   *Source J tells us that some mills were dusty and dangerous to work in.*
    Source K tells us that some mills were well ventilated and clean.

> **REMEMBER: To get full marks you need to write down evidence from more than one source. You may find three pieces of relevant evidence in Source K – the source also tells you that the mill at Inverbervie had low roofs in the rooms. – but you must add another piece of evidence from Source J or L to get all four marks.**

6   *I have found that working conditions were not the same in all mills. Some mills were bad but others were very nice to work in.*

OR

Working conditions were probably bad in most mills because two sources show this, but there were some good ones.

> **REMEMBER: In this answer do not just repeat what you have said in question 5 – you will not get any marks if you do. You must try to say what you think you have found out about working conditions in mills in general from the sources.**

Now here is an investigation for you to try:
In Questions 7, 8 and 9 the topic for investigating is: The Suffragettes

Study the information in the sources, and then answer the questions which follow.
In Source L a Suffragette leader, Emmeline Pankhurst, describes how women were treated around 1900.

Source L
I was shocked to be reminded over and over again how little respect there was in the world for women and children. I found out that men teachers received more money than women teachers although women had to do extra work. It was clear men regarded women as servants.

7   *Source L is useful evidence about why women wanted to be able to vote? Give two reasons why it is useful.*   2 marks

Source M describes some of the activities carried out by Suffragettes.

Source M
They damaged public buildings and set fire to letter boxes. At Moray Golf Club in Lossiemouth the Prime Minister was seriously assaulted by two young Suffragettes.

In Source N a Suffragette who was arrested explains how she was treated for refusing to eat.

Source N

I was held down and a long tube with a funnel on the end was forced up my nose. I felt great pain. My ear drums seemed to be bursting. Then the doctor holding the funnel poured milk or egg and milk into it. I was very sick.

8   *What does Source M tell you about Suffragettes?*
      What does Source N tell you about Suffragettes?   4 marks
9   *Write down your findings about the Suffragettes.*   2 marks

A final reminder about all Enquiry Skills questions. The evidence you need to answer these questions is ALWAYS in the sources you are given and what you are told about them. All you need to do is to look carefully for it, as you have been taught to do.

G *General level*

Most people who sit Foundation level in the final examination will also attempt General level. When you see the examination paper at this level you will notice three big differences from the Foundation level examination paper:

- You do not write your answers on the examination paper but in a separate booklet.
- The question paper has many more pages than the Foundation level paper.
- Each context in the General paper is divided into Section A (Knowledge and Understanding) and Section B (Enquiry Skills).

The Enquiry Skills needed at General level are largely the same as at Foundation level but have some important bits added to them. There is also one skill introduced at General level which is not required at Foundation level.

So the list of Enquiry Skills for General level looks like this. You will be able to:

1   decide for yourself if a source is or is not valuable, useful or reliable;
2   explain the point of view shown by a source;
3   compare two sources;
4   find and organise relevant evidence from two or more sources;
5   provide your own conclusion on an issue, using what you have found from sources you are given AND your own knowledge;
6   show that you know something about what was going on at the time a primary source was actually produced.

The extra things you have to do at General level will be explained as we work through these six skills. You should also expect the sources you have to work with to be longer and a bit more difficult.

It is very likely you will have relevant evidence from your own memory to use even where it is not asked for. Do not hesitate to use it **except in those investigation questions which ask you to find and write down evidence from sources.**

1   *Deciding on the value of a source*

In this type of question at General level you will be looking for the same kind of evidence as at Foundation level – and at Credit level too – BUT you will not have any help in the question as to whether the source is valuable/useful or not.

You have to decide for yourself AND give good reasons for your decision. Here is an example to help you understand.

Source A appeared in a German newspaper when the Treaty of Versailles was signed.

Source A

VENGEANCE GERMAN NATION!
Today in Versailles a disgraceful treaty is being signed .
Never forget it! German honour is dragged to the grave.
The German people will push forward to regain that place
among nations to which they are entitled. There will be
vengeance for the shame of 1919.

Is Source A useful as evidence of German reaction to the Treaty of Versailles? Give reasons for your answer.

3 marks

The first thing you need to decide is if you think this source is useful evidence or not and then write that down as the start of your answer. You can always get full marks either way IF you produce relevant evidence.

Then add **three** reasons to support your decision. In this case you will get full marks for an answer like this.

Source A is useful evidence because it is a primary source written on the same day as the treaty was signed. Also it comes from a German newspaper. It shows what some Germans thought of the treaty.

You would also obtain full marks if you were a little cautious about the usefulness of the source and your answer looked like this.

Source A is quite useful as evidence because it is a primary source written on the same day as the treaty was signed. But it comes from a German newspaper which might be trying to stir up feelings in Germany against the treaty. It only shows some Germans wanted to oppose the treaty.

REMEMBER: At General level you do not get a mark for just saying that a source is primary or secondary – you have to add more evidence to show, for example, that it is very close to the event it describes OR that it is by someone directly involved in the event to obtain a mark.

Now here is a source for you to evaluate:

Source B is what Hitler shouted when he learned that a communist had set fire to the German Parliament buildings in 1933.

Source B

Every Communist official must be shot. All Communist deputies must be hanged this very night. All friends of the Communists must be locked up!

1   *Is Source B valuable evidence about the way Hitler treated his opponents? Give reasons for your answer.*

                                                            3 marks

2   *Explaining the point of view in a source*

This is a more advanced form of the same skill needed at Foundation level. At this level you will not be told the point of view of the source but will have to decide this for yourself. The source you are given to work with will be more complicated and probably longer.

Here is an example to help you:

Source C is a telegram from General Rodzianko to the Tsar in March 1917.

Source C

The position is serious. Law and order has collapsed in the capital. The government is paralysed. The transportation of food and fuel is completely disorganised. The general dissatisfaction grows. Disorderly firing takes place in the streets. A person trusted by the country must form a new government immediately.

What is Rodzianko's view of the position of the Tsar's government in March 1917? Give evidence to support your answer.

                                                            3 marks

Look at the question carefully to see what you are being asked to find out about. In this case it is Rodzianko's view on how secure the Tsar's government was in 1917.

Read the introduction to the source, but pay much more attention to what is in the source itself. Rodzianko clearly thinks the Tsar's government is in danger and you should write this first. Then add three pieces of evidence to support you opinion. Your answer would look like this.

In Source C Rodzianko thinks the Tsar's government is in danger. He says a new government is needed, under someone the people trust. He believes this is necessary because law and order has broken down and there is widespread unrest.

An alternative answer could be,

In Source C Rodzianko thinks the Tsar's government is in danger. He says a new government is needed, under someone the people trust. He believes this is necessary because the existing government can not do anything, and that essentials like food are not reaching people.

REMEMBER: Decide on the view given in the source and then choose evidence from the source to support your decision. DO NOT just copy out everything the source says.

Here is an example for you to try:

Source D is part of a comment on Stalin written by Lenin in 1923.

Source D

Stalin is too rude and this defect is unacceptable in a General Secretary. That is why I suggest that comrades think of ways of removing Stalin from his post and appointing another man who is more tolerant, more loyal, more polite and more considerate.

2   *What is Lenin's opinion of Stalin as a future leader of Russia? Give reasons for your answer.*

3 marks

3   *Comparing two sources*

You will be given two sources to study. They will both be about the same thing. They may agree OR disagree in the evidence they provide and this is the first decision you need to make.

Read the introduction to each of the sources carefully because this will probably suggest what the question is going to be about. The sources:-
- may both be primary sources;
- may both be secondary sources;
- may be one of each;
- one may be written and the other a picture.

Here is an example to help you:

Both these sources are about a German air raid on Clydebank, near Glasgow.

Source E is a photograph of Clydebank taken on the 14th of March 1941.

Source E

Source F is from William Anderson's book *A Memory of the Clydebank Blitz.*

Source F

About four in the morning the all-clear sounded . Most wardens went home but a few volunteers were needed to go to the bombed area. The truck which took us to Clydebank crunched all the way through broken glass. We saw tenements cut in half and had to detour past smouldering ruins. Above all we had to witness the shock of the folk walking aimlessly down the middle of the street.

Do Sources E and F agree about the effects of the German air raid on Clydebank? 3 marks

Look at the two sources carefully. They seem to agree about several things to do with the air raid. So your answer should look like this:

The sources do agree about the effects of the air raid. Source E shows the road full of bits of buildings and Source F says the truck drove through a lot of broken glass. Source E shows tenements in ruins and Source F describes tenements cut in half. Source E shows smoke still coming from burning houses and Source F says ruins were still burning.

You could add to your answer that Source E shows people working on the buildings and Source F says volunteers came to help after the raid.

REMEMBER: Give the evidence you are comparing in full if you want to be certain of getting all the marks. DO NOT just say something like – *The sources agree because both show there were ruined buildings.*

Now here is a comparison for you to try:

These two sources are about inflation in Germany in the 1920s.

Source G is from a book about Germany in the 1920s by Louis L. Snyder.

Source G

Widows, civil servants, teachers, army officers and pensioners lost their lifetime savings because of inflation. It was a scar that never healed. These were the people who later rejected democratic government and turned to Adolf Hitler.

Source H is from a recent book about life in Germany during the 1920s.

Source H

His savings, his wife's savings, their plot of land and all their hopes vanished into thin air overnight. With his savings he was able to buy just one cup and saucer to give as a wedding present to his wife. The loss of his bank account shattered any faith he had in democratic government and struck at his self–respect and his right to be respected.

3   Do Sources G and H agree about the effects of inflation on Germany in the 1920s?   3 marks

> **REMEMBER: All the evidence you need to answer this type of question is in the sources you are given. If one source is primary and the other is secondary you may even be able to use this fact to gain a mark – for example, if the question just asks you to compare the sources as evidence about a person or event.**

Enquiry Skills 4 and 5 are part of **Investigating** and you will only be asked questions needing these skills in Unit I contexts. You will find Section B questions in the Unit I context you are attempting, are all about Investigating an issue – that is something about which it is possible to have different opinions. Here is an example of an investigation to help you see what you need to do.

SECTION B: ENQUIRY SKILLS

The issue for investigating is: The Highland Clearances of the 1820s were justified and necessary. Study the sources carefully and answer the questions which follow.
You should use your own knowledge where appropriate.

Source I is a description of the eviction of crofters in 1819, written by someone who was evicted and wrote about it some 20 years later.

Source I

I saw big groups quickly set fire to the houses until about three hundred were in flames. The alarm and confusion were enormous. Little or no time was given to remove people or their property.

Men struggled to save the sick and helpless before fire reached them. The fire lasted six days until all the houses were destroyed.

3   *Is Source I reliable evidence about how people were evicted in the Highlands? Give reasons for your answer.*   3 marks

REMEMBER: In this case look for information to help your answer in what you are told about the source, as well as in the source itself.

Decide if you think you can trust the evidence in the source – and if so how far – and then give three reasons to support your decision. So your answer might look like this:

I don't think this is reliable evidence. It is not really a primary source because it was written 20 years after the event. The author probably hated evictions because it had happened to him. He is very biased and may have exaggerated what happened.

OR

I think this is quite reliable evidence because the writer actually saw what happened. He probably hated evictions because it had happened to him. Also he wrote some time after the events and may have exaggerated them in his memory.

Both these answers should gain full marks.

Source J gives a landlord's view of the crofters in Sutherland in 1820.

Source J

The men did not like regular work and left the heavy labour to the women. They spent most of their time in idleness or making illegal alcohol. They were content with the most simple and poorest food. The cattle they reared were of the poorest kind.

The coast of Sutherland has many different types of fish, more than enough to eat and to sell in other markets. It seemed the most natural thing to rear sheep in the mountains and send the crofters to the coast to live.

Source K is a description of conditions in part of the Highlands and was written in 1840.

Source K

The population was growing rapidly and the means of supporting each family were becoming less. Poverty was increasing quickly because the price of cattle was falling, the herring fisheries were failing and there was serious unemployment.

4   *What evidence in Source J agrees with the view evictions were justified and necessary?*
     What evidence in Source K disagrees with the view that evictions were justified and necessary?
                                                                                                    5 marks

REMEMBER: An issue is something on which people are likely to have different opinions. This means you are likely to find conflicting evidence in the sources.

The two sources for question 4 do not obviously contradict one another, but look at them again carefully. Your answer should have five pieces of evidence and look like this.

Source J says that crofters were lazy and did not try to make their crofts successful. It also says that they could do much better at the coast. It says that the natural thing to put in the mountains was sheep. (3 points)

Source K says the reason crofters were not successful was that the population was becoming too big. It also says that fishing had failed. It says that they were poor because there were no jobs for them to do. (3 points – only two needed)

REMEMBER: Just write down the relevant evidence from each source. DO NOT try to compare the sources.

5   *Do you agree that the Highland Clearances of the 1820s were justified and necessary? Use evidence from the sources AND your own knowledge to come to a conclusion.*   4 marks

REMEMBER: You must give a conclusion based on evidence from the sources. To get full marks you must use at least ONE piece of relevant evidence from your own memory as well.

Your answer should be something like this:

I think new methods of farming had to be tried in the Highlands. Many new methods of farming were being tried in Britain at that time, like enclosures. This meant crofters would need to change their ways or leave their land. Because the population was growing fast many might have left anyway, without being evicted. So change was needed but some of the ways it was done were bad.

This answer uses evidence from each of the sources and one piece not from the sources – about new farming methods in Britain.

Now here is an investigation for you to try.

SECTION B: ENQUIRY SKILLS

The issue for investigating is: The benefits brought by the growth of railways in the middle of the nineteenth century outweighed any problems it caused.
Study the sources carefully and answer the questions which follow.
You should use your own knowledge where appropriate.

Source L is an entry from the year 1830 in William Dyott's *Diary 1781–1845*.

Source L
I took a seat at Liverpool in the mail coach to London. One of the other passengers from Coventry

was a person employed in survey work on the line of a railway from Birmingham to London. It will be a most important work and, if it is built, it will make highways, horses and canals all useless.

6   *How useful is Source L as evidence about the effects of railway building?*   3 marks

Source M is also from William Dyott's *Diary*. This is an entry from the year 1837.

Source M
We left Birmingham at half-past eleven and arrived at Liverpool at four o'clock exactly without any trouble. The train stopped at different stations for five minutes just to deliver and collect passengers and parcels. The speed is so great it is hardly possible to see details of the countryside as you pass. The railways to Manchester and Birmingham must add greatly to the wealth of Liverpool.

In Source N Samuel Smiles describes opposition to railways. This was written in 1857.

Source N
When Colonel Sibthorpe stated his hatred of railways, he only expressed the feelings of the country gentry and many of the middle classes in the South. The MP for Cheltenham protested about the railways running through the heart of hunting property. Other critics talked about the noise and nuisance caused by locomotives and the danger of fire to nearby property. They said innkeepers would be ruined, the stagecoach destroyed forever, landowners and farmers reduced to poverty.

7   *What were the benefits brought by railways according to Source M?*
     What problems did railways cause according to Source N?   5 marks
8   *Do you agree that the benefits brought by railways outweighed any problems they caused?*
     Use evidence from the sources AND your own knowledge to come to a conclusion.   4 marks

6   *Showing that you can relate a source to other information on the topic*

REMEMBER: This skill is only examined at General and Credit levels and in Units II and III. In this type of question you will have to use information from your own memory to answer the question successfully. You will always be reminded of this in the question.

Here is an example of the kind of question which tests this skill:
Source O is a poster issued by the British Government during the First World War.

Source O

How typical is Source O of ways the British Government tried to protect food supplies during the First World War. You should use your own knowledge and give reasons for your answer. 3 marks

First of all you need to decide if you think this poster and what it does are things the Government often tried to do during the war. Some of the evidence you can use comes from the poster but at least ONE piece of evidence must come from your memory. The following answer would have gained full marks.

This poster is typical of ways the Government tried to protect food supplies during the war. It is propaganda and the government used a lot of this. It is also meant for all civilians and the Government expected them to help the war effort. The Government also tried to help food supplies in other ways, for example by getting women to work on farms in place of men.

OR

This poster is typical of propaganda used by the Government. There were also other posters about food such as 'We risk our lives to bring you food. Don't waste it'. But the Government also tried to get more food by asking women to work on farms in place of men who had gone to fight. Also the navy set up a convoy system to stop losses to U-boats.

Notice that in the second answer almost all the evidence comes from memory and not from the source. This is an acceptable answer as long as you relate the evidence you use to the question.

Here is an example for you to try:

Source P is from a speech by Rudolph Hess at a Nazi rally in 1934.

Source P

The party is Hitler. Hitler is Germany just as Germany is Hitler. Heil Hitler!

9 *Is Source P typical of ways the Nazi Party tried to win support for Hitler? You should use your own knowledge and give reasons for your answer.* 3 marks

C Credit level

The Credit level examination paper will look similar to the one you sat at General level and may even have fewer pages than the General, but you still write your answers in a separate booklet. If you are attempting the Credit paper you should also be sitting General level. The six Enquiry Skills are the same at these two levels. Here is the list again to remind you of what you are expected to be able to do:

1 decide for yourself if a source is or is not valuable, useful or reliable;
2 explain the point of view shown by a source;
3 compare the evidence in several sources;
4 find and organise relevant evidence from two or more sources;
5 provide your own conclusion on an issue, using what you have found from sources you are given AND your own knowledge;
6 show that you know something about what was going on at the time a primary source was actually produced.

The differences between the two levels are:
- the sources at credit level are more difficult;
- more careful evaluation of evidence is expected in the answers you give.

As at General level all the Enquiry Skills questions will be in Section B. In Unit I contexts – as at General level – your enquiry will take the form of an **investigation** into an issue, which will be given to you at the start of each Section B.

REMEMBER: For most of the questions in Section B all the evidence you need to obtain full marks will be contained in the sources you are given and the introductions to them. Where you need to use your own knowledge to get full marks, this will be clearly shown in the question.

It is very likely you will have relevant evidence from your own memory to use, even where it is not asked for. Do not hesitate to use it **except in the investigation questions which ask you to find and organise evidence from sources.**

Now let's look at the first Enquiry Skill.

1 Deciding on the value of a source or sources

In Units II and III you will be carrying out the same task as at General level – often with the same type of evidence. That is to say, you will be looking for relevant evidence in the introduction and in the source itself. As at General level, you will not get a mark just for saying that a source is primary or secondary unless you add a relevant comment – for example about who wrote it or about the date it was produced.

In the Unit 1 Section B Investigations, you will find there are TWO sources for you to evaluate. You can either write about them separately **or** you can compare them as evidence, for example:–

- if they are both by people who were present at the events described in the sources then you can say both are valuable because they are eyewitness accounts;
- if they are both by important politicians you can say they valuable because of their authorship.

Here is an example of a straightforward source evaluation:

Source A is from the *Daily Record* of the 8th May 1918.

Source A

PEACE TREATY FOR GERMANY
STERN BUT JUST
THE ALLIES' TERMS

The Germans were presented with the Allied Peace Treaty at Versailles yesterday afternoon. The meeting did not last an hour. M. Clemenceau said that the Germans had asked for peace and the Allies were ready to give it. But, he added the Treaty had been bought at too high a price to allow the Allies to do other than guard against another war.

The German delegate rejected the suggestion that Germany alone was responsible for the war.

How useful is Source A as evidence about the Treaty of Versailles?   4 marks

The introduction to the source gives some useful information in this case. It tells you two things you can use

- that the source is from a British newspaper;
- that it comes from the time the treaty was signed.

The rest of your answer comes from the source itself and should look like this.

This report is quite useful for several reasons. It is a primary source, published at almost the same time as the treaty was being discussed. It only shows part of the allies view on the terms of peace. Although it is from a British paper it does not give a view obviously biased against the Germans. In fact, it shows some of what Germans did not like in the treaty. But, the newspaper was trying to convince people that the treaty was fair and good.

To show the source is **quite useful** this answer has used the information from the introduction about when the report appeared and where. It has commented on the content of the source by noting it gives **part** of the Allies' peace terms. The fact it is from a British paper is used first to say the report is not very anti-German and that a German view was included; then to note from the headline that the paper was suggesting this was a fair treaty.

So this answer gives a **balanced** view of the usefulness of the source – showing it has some value but noting at least two possible weaknesses:

- it only gives part of the Allies' view;
- the answer notes the paper is trying to persuade people the Treaty is fair.

REMEMBER: At Credit level you must say what you think clearly, BUT part of your answer should show that you recognise when there is a weakness or something missing from source evidence, as well as giving its strengths.

Here is a source for you to evaluate:

Source B is part of a broadcast to the American people on 22 October 1961, by President John F Kennedy.

Source B

This government has maintained the closest surveillance of the Soviet military build-up on the island of Cuba. Within the last week, unmistakable evidence has established the fact that a series of offensive missile sites is now in preparation on that imprisoned island. The purpose of these bases can be none other than to provide a nuclear strike capability against the West.

1   *How useful is Source B as evidence about American reactions to Soviet missile bases on Cuba?*

4 marks

2   *Explain the point(s) of view in a source*

The source you are given will probably be longer and certainly more complicated than sources you worked with on this skill at General level. You may also find the questions you are asked about point of view of a source, encourage you to discuss what you see in the source, rather than just asking you to identify the point of view.

All the information you need to obtain full marks is in the source and the introduction to it. So read them carefully. Here is an example:

Source C is a view on poor relief, written by Professor McGill in 1819.

Source C

The poor may be persons who are able to supply what they need by labour but are unwilling to do so. They are not entitled to receive the assistance of charity. They are able to supply their own wants, if they choose, and to assist them in any way is to give direct encouragement to idleness.

There may be persons who are weak in body or mind and are unable to provide for themselves. These are the people the law mainly meant to help.

Discuss the view of poor relief in Source C.

4 marks

The introduction gives some information which may be useful evidence but almost all the answer will come from the source itself.

> *This view is interesting but comes from quite early in the nineteenth century and is the view of one man, who may be quite well informed as he is a professor. He is not very sympathetic towards the poor. He says they may be people who just do not want to work. In fact he thinks it would be wrong to help these people because it would make them even lazier. He does think there are some people who deserve help because they are sick and unable to work.*

This answer has made full use of information from the introduction, to suggest being careful about the importance of the views in the source.
The rest of the answer comes from the source and

- makes a clear statement about the unsympathetic view of the poor in the source;
- shows awareness that the author of the source is willing to admit some people may deserve poor relief.

There is **balance** in the evaluation made in the answer to the questions, and this is something you want to try to include in your answers.

An example for you to try is given below:
Source D comes from the writings of Joseph Stalin.

Source D
Maintaining the rule of the people is impossible without a Communist Party which is strongly united and has iron discipline. The Party is the instrument of the people. It is strengthened by purging itself of those who try to take advantage of it, because these are the people who divide the Party. Our Party succeeded because it was able to purge itself of such people.

2   *What is Stalin's view of the Communist Party as shown in Source D?*   4 marks

3   *Compare the evidence in several sources*

Usually, as at General level, you will be comparing evidence from two sources. The sources will be about the same topic and may agree or disagree. Both sources may be written or one may be a picture.
Your best approach is to read the question which asks you to compare the sources before you try to study them in detail – NOTE that it may be the second not the first question after the sources. (Often the first question after the sources will ask about the value or usefulness of one of them.)
When you read the question you will know what to look for in the sources. This may be

- agreement between sources;
- disagreement between sources;
- a certain amount of agreement/disagreement between sources.

So this question can appear in different ways, for instance:
- *Compare the evidence in Sources A and B about . . .*
- *Do Sources A and B agree about . . .?*
- *To what extent do sources A and B disagree about . . .?*

In every case the evidence you need will be in the sources you are given and sometimes there will also be useful information in the source introductions. Here is an example:

Sources E and F are both about reform of Parliament.

Source E is from a speech made by the Duke of Wellington in the House of Lords in 1830.

Source E

For myself I will go further and say that I have never read or heard of any way that representation can be improved which satisfies my mind. I will go further and say that Parliament and the system of representation possess the full and entire confidence of the country.

Source F comes from the *Declaration of the Birmingham Political Union* also in 1830.

Source F

The House of Commons in its present state is too distant from the wants and interests of the lower and middle classes of the people. The great aristocratic interests of all kinds are well represented there. But the interests of Industry and Trade have scarcely any representatives at all.

Do Sources E and F agree about the need for reform of Parliament? 4 marks

By reading the question before you study the sources carefully you learn that you are looking for evidence about Reform of Parliament. When you read the sources it very quickly becomes clear they do not agree at all and it is sensible to write this first. Then look for actual pieces of evidence which disagree.

> *Sources E and F do not agree at all about the need to reform Parliament. The writer of E thinks that Parliament has the support of everyone but in Source F it says there are many who are not happy with representation. In Source E the writer claims Parliament has the full confidence of the country and in F it says Industry and Trade are hardly represented at all. Source E gives an aristocratic's view on reform while F is giving the opinions of working and middle class people.*

REMEMBER: Write what you think about agreement between the sources clearly at the start of your answer. Then show the evidence in full from both sources which has helped you decide. If you just write 'Source F is for reform and Source E is not' you will not get marks.

Your answer could have been slightly more detailed if you had been asked to *Compare the evidence about reform of Parliament in Sources E and F.* In that case you could also have said that both E and F are primary sources from close to the time of reform and that one was written by an aristocrat and the other probably by someone from the middle class.

Here is a comparison for you to try:

Sources G and H are about life in Russia under the Five Year Plans.
Source G was written in 1937 by someone who worked in Russia.

Source G

About 550 men and women lived in a wooden structure about 800 feet long and 15 feet wide. The room contained approximately 500 narrow beds, covered with mattresses filled with straw. There were no blankets. Some time later I visited a four storey brick structure about three years old but badly built. In this building lived about 150 families split into groups of 15 families, which had one room each and shared one kitchen and one toilet.

Source H was written in 1938 by Sir Walter Citrine.

Source H

There are large tenements, badly built and sometimes five storeys high. They have no baths and usually only cold water. There are few, if any, ways to wash clothes. A wash basin or a separate bath-room is the exception and not the rule. I never saw a separate toilet for one family. They were all shared with another family or two. Against this I must say that rents are very low and the houses are usually centrally heated.

3   *Do Sources G and H agree about living conditions in Russia in the 1930s?*   5 marks

As at General level, Enquiry Skills 4 and 5 are part of **Investigating** and you will only be asked questions needing these skills in Unit I contexts. You will find Section B questions in the Unit I context you are attempting are all about **Investigating** an issue – that is something about which it is possible to have different opinions.

Here is an example of an investigation to help you see what you need to do.

SECTION B: ENQUIRY SKILLS

The issue for investigating is: The reform of parliament in 1832 was a major step towards democracy.

Study the sources carefully and answer the questions which follow.

You should use your own knowledge where appropriate.

Source A is from *A Representative History of Great Britain and Ireland* by THB Oldfield, published in 1816.

Source A

The 33 counties return only 30 Members of Parliament, six having the right of sending an MP to every second parliament. When the county of Caithness elects a member, he is chosen by Sir John Sinclair. Lord Melville always boasted that he could select 39 out of the 45 MPs who represented the whole kingdom of Scotland.

Source B is from the *Report of the Select Committee on Bribery at Elections* written in 1835.

Source B

Question	Have you ever known intimidation to be practised to any extent at a county election?
Answer	Yes, by landlords over tenants.
Question	In what ways have they exercised that intimidation?
Answer	By insisting that they voted as the landlord wished or they would lose their farms.

Source C is from the Reform Act of 1832.

Source C

It is necessary to take effective measures to correct various abuses in the election of Members to the House of Commons that have existed for a long time. To take MPs from many very small places and give them to large, wealthy towns. To extend the franchise to many of his majesty's subjects who have not been able to vote before. To reduce the costs of elections.

In every city or borough which elects an MP or MPs to serve in any future Parliament every male person of full age who owns or rents any property with an annual rental value of more than £10 shall be entitled to vote.

How useful are Sources A and B for investigating the importance of reform of parliament in 1832?

4 marks

What evidence in the sources supports the view that reform of parliament in 1832 was a major step towards democracy?

What evidence in the sources suggest that reform of parliament in 1832 was not a major step towards democracy?

6 marks

How important was the reform of parliament in 1832? You should use evidence from the sources AND your own knowledge to come to a balanced conclusion.

5 marks

REMEMBER: An issue is something on which people are likely to have different opinions. This means you are likely to find conflicting evidence in the sources.

At Credit level you will probably be asked about the usefulness or value of TWO sources to an investigation. You can

- write about each source separately;
- write about both sources together;
- do a little bit of both of the above.

Look at the marks given for the question and do not write too much about the sources for this question. DO NOT try to make a detailed comparison of the two sources – they may be very different – as this is NOT what you are expected to do.

The next question asks you find and write down relevant information from the sources.

The final question expects you to write a conclusion which shows that

- you understand the issue you are investigating;
- have considered evidence from all sources which suggests the possibility of at least two different conclusions;
- have added evidence from your memory to what you have found in the sources and clearly offered your own conclusion on the issue.

Now here are some examples of answers to the three questions.

- *Source A is a primary source but was written 16 years before the Reform Act was passed. It gives useful evidence about elections to parliament before reform. It was written to show reform was needed but it does not give any useful information about the effects of the 1832 reform. (3 marks gained so far).*

  Source B is also a primary source from much nearer the actual reform of parliament. It comes from a committee investigating elections and is likely to have accurate information. It shows there were still problems after the reform of 1832. (at least another 2 marks).

- *It was a major step towards democracy because Source C shows that MPs from small places were to be given to the large towns and that election costs were to be lower, meaning more people could afford to take part. It also shows more men in towns were going to be able to vote. (3 – perhaps 4 marks)*

- *It was not a major step to democracy because Source C also shows only men could vote and only men who had a certain amount of money. Also Source B shows that even after the reform there were still problems at elections. (3 marks)*

- *The reform of parliament in 1832 was a not a major step towards democracy. It did make some changes, for example to help some of the towns and to give the vote to more men. But it did not allow women to vote <u>and this change did not come until the twentieth century</u>. It also did not stop landlords forcing some people to vote the way they wanted, <u>because voting was still done in public.</u> It was important because it showed reform was possible but it did not bring democracy.*

OR

- *The reform of parliament in 1832 was a major step towards democracy. It gave more MPs to the towns and took them from smaller places <u>like some of the rotten boroughs which sometimes had no people living in them.</u> It <u>gave encouragement to the new industrial towns that they might soon get their own MPs.</u> It gave the vote to more men than had been able to vote before. It showed that reform was possible even though it did not cure problems like intimidation at elections or give the vote to women.*

The <u>underlining</u> shows where information has been included which is **not** in the sources.

Either of the above answers should get full marks, but remember you must have at least ONE piece of evidence from your own memory in your conclusion.

Now here is an investigation for you to try:

SECTION B: ENQUIRY SKILLS

The issue for investigating is: Trade Unions grew greatly in strength between the 1880s and the 1920s.

Study the sources carefully and answer the questions which follow.

You should use your own knowledge where appropriate.

Source A is part of a report on the dock strike from *The Times* of 16 September 1889.

Source A

The dock labourers and their allies have won a remarkable victory. The dock companies have granted all their demands. The strike will be a most significant event in the relations between employers and workers. There is first the fact that the dock labourers have been able to combine, although they have no special skill, industry or strength. Combination has previously been considered a weapon only available to the skilled labourer.

The case of the dock labourers took a powerful hold on public opinion. It drew sympathy and material support from all quarters, from Australia above all.

Source B comes from a description of the effects of the Taff Vale Decision in 1901. It is taken from *Industrial Democracy* by S and B Webb, published in 1916.

Source B

The judgement makes no change in the lawfulness of Trade Unionism. No act is made wrongful which was not wrongful before. If a Trade Union causes damage, it seems fair it should be liable for what it has done. The grievance of the Trade Unions lies in the uncertainty of English law. This is increased by the dislike of Trade Unionism which nearly all judges and juries share with the rest of the upper and middle classes.

The middle classes are more hostile to Trade Unionism than a generation ago. When Trade Unionism was struggling for legal recognition, it seemed only fair that the workmen should be put in a position to make a good fight against the employers. Accordingly strikes and peaceful picketing were legalised. Gradually this has given way to the view that a stoppage of work by an industrial dispute is a public nuisance which ought to be prevented by the Government.

Source C is a description of the Triple Alliance formed in 1914. It comes from Robert Smillie *The Labour Year Book, 1916.*

Source C

One result of the industrial unrest of recent years is the Triple Industrial Alliance. The miners had a meeting with the representatives of the two industries most comparable to their own – railways and transport. The three bodies have much in common. Their membership is large. A strike on the railway system affects the miners and transport workers.

The new body is not to be a rival to any other. Action is to be confined to joint national action. The main idea is that each of these great fighting organisations, before embarking on any movement, should submit its proposals to the others and that action should be taken on joint proposals.

3   *How useful are Source A and B for investigating the strength of Trade Unions between the 1880s and the 1920s?*   4 marks

4   *What evidence is there in the sources to support the view that Trade Unions did grow much stronger between the 1880s and 1920s?*
    *What evidence is there in the sources that Trade Unions did **not** grow stronger between the 1880s and 1920s?*   6 marks

5   *Do you agree that Trade Unions grew much stronger between the 1880s and the 1920s? You should use evidence from the sources and your own knowledge to come to a balanced conclusion.*   5 marks

6   Show you can relate a source(s) to other information on the topic

This is the same skill you needed at General level. Questions asking you to use this skill may be based on more than one source but will only appear in Units II and III. What is expected at Credit level is that you will be able to show more understanding of the background in which the source(s) were produced.

REMEMBER: You will need to use some information from your memory in this type of question. You will be reminded of this in the question itself.

The question may appear as

How fully do the sources describe the events of . . . ?   OR
Are these sources typical of . . . ?

Here is an example:
Source D is from a German government report in 1930.

Source D
Frequently propaganda squads stay in a certain place for several days and try to win the population for the Nazi movement through the most varied sorts of entertainment, such as concerts, sports days and even church parades.

Source E is a photograph of a Nazi rally.

Source E

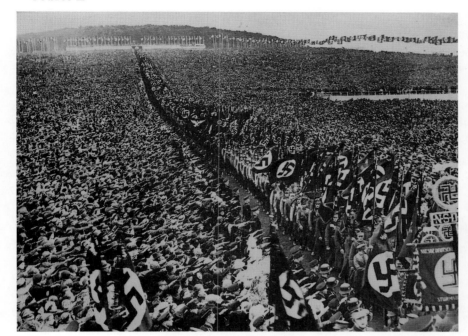

How fully do Sources D and E show how the Nazi party tried to win support in Germany? You should use your own knowledge and give reasons for your answer.

4 marks

OR

Do Sources D and E describe typical Nazi propaganda activities? You should use your own knowledge and give reasons for your answer.   4 marks

In the first form of the question you are asked to make a judgement about the evidence, in terms of how much it tells you about Nazi attempts to win support. You can be certain the answer expected is that there is some major information missing. So your answer should look like this.

> *Sources D and F do not fully show how the Nazi party tried to win support. Source D does describe things such as the fun activities put on by the Nazis to get people to join. Source E shows the way the Nazis used great parades and uniforms and flags to influence people. <u>The sources do not mention the way the Nazis beat up people who did not support them. They do not show how they used the radio to put out Nazi propaganda or how they changed school books to make children want to support the Nazis.</u> So the sources give a lot of evidence but leave a lot out.*

Your own memory has provided additional evidence – underlined in the answer. The last sentence gives a little more balance to the answer. In the second form of the question you are also asked for a judgement, but in this case the answer expected would be that the sources do describe typical Nazi propaganda activities. Again you should begin by saying this, so your answer would look like this.

> *The sources do show typical Nazi propaganda activities. They show the way they used fun activities to get people interested and they also show the big parades the Nazi often used. <u>The Nazis organised groups for young people to join, like the Hitler Youth for boys or the German Maidens for girls and they went on camps and played sports and marched. Even the young people had to wear military style uniforms like the ones in Source E.</u>*

Again, evidence not from the sources is underlined in the answer.

Now here is an example for you to try:

Source F is part of a speech about collectivisation by a Communist Party official to a crowd of peasants.

Source F

Isn't it about time you stopped thinking each one for himself and his own piggish hide? You kulaks of course will never become reconciled to a new order. you love to fatten on other people's blood. We'll wipe you off the face of the earth.

Source G is a photograph of a peasant march in favour of collectivisation in the 1930s.

Source G

The inscription on the banner reads 'We demand collectivisation and the liquidation of the Kulaks as a class'.

6 Do Sources F and G fully show the attitude to Collectivisation in Russia in the 1930s? You should use your own knowledge and give reasons for your answer.   4 marks

OR

7 Do Sources F and G show typical attitudes towards collectivisation in the 1930s? You should use your own knowledge and give reasons for your answer.

4 marks

Answers to Sample Questions

F Foundation level

Question 1 Source B is useful because it is a primary source,
because it is by an eyewitness,
because it tells you what machine guns did.

Question 2   He thinks they were weak.
            He thinks they disagreed among themselves.

Question 3   Source G says it was fun.
            Source H says it was boring.
            Source G says there was a lot going on.
            Source H says they stood about just listening to speeches.

Investigating

Question 7   Source L is useful because it is by an important Suffragette leader and because it tells you why women felt they were badly treated.

Question 8   Source M tells you they attacked buildings and they even attacked the Prime Minister.
            Source N tells you how badly they were treated in prison and that they were forced to eat.

Question 9   I found out that they thought women were not treated the same as men and that they tried to get things improved by attacking public buildings and politicians. (OR – that they were arrested and badly treated.)

G *General level*

Question 1   Yes it is valuable because it is a primary source by Hitler himself. It shows what he thought of communists and that he meant to make all Germans turn against them.

Question 2   Lenin does not think Stalin should become leader of Russia. He thinks Stalin is too rough and that the leader of Russia must be more of a politician. He also thinks Stalin is not willing to listen to what others want.

Question 3   The sources do agree very well about the effects of inflation. Source G says people lost their savings and Source H also says they lost their savings. Source G says people were deeply hurt by their losses and Source H says he even lost his self-respect. Both Source G and Source H say that people turned against democratic government.

Investigating

Question 6   Source L is useful as evidence about the effects of the railways because it describes what they will do to other forms of transport. The evidence is from someone who was alive when the first railways were being planned so he does not know what they will do to roads and canals and is only giving his opinion. Also we do not know anything else about the author but he seems to approve of railway building.

Question 7   Source M says that railways will make travel fast. It says they are reliable. It says they can pick up and drop off passengers and parcels quickly. (OR It says they can make towns rich.) Source N says the railways annoyed the country landowners. It says they interfere with hunting. It says they are dangerous to property. (OR It says they annoyed people because of their noise. It says inns and stagecoaches would lose money.)

REMEMBER: You only need FIVE pieces of evidence in total.

Question 8   Yes I do think the benefits of the railways were better than the problems they caused. They made travel a lot faster. They could carry people and goods better than coaches or canal boats. They increased the wealth of towns like Liverpool. <u>I also know that they allowed food like fish to reach places away from the ports and remain fresh.</u>

> **REMEMBER: The underlined evidence is definitely not in the sources and you must have at least ONE piece of evidence from your memory in this answer.**

Question 9   Source P is typical of ways the Nazi party tried to win support for Hitler. The Nazis organised many rallies at which Hitler was glorified. Hitler was treated as the one leader of Germany by the Nazis. <u>Also the Nazis tried to make it impossible for anyone to oppose Hitler by making claims like this and by sending any opponents to concentration camps.</u>

> **REMEMBER: The underlined evidence is definitely not in the sources and you must have at least ONE piece of evidence from your memory in this answer.**

C *Credit level*

Question 1   Source B is very useful as evidence about American reactions because it is a primary source from the actual time the missile bases were being built. Also it comes from the President, who should speak for America. It shows the great worry the American government had over the missile bases. But the way it is written may be biased because he was trying to persuade Americans that there was a real danger from the bases.

Question 2   Source D shows that Stalin thought the Communist Party was needed to make the rule of the people happen. He thought the Party had to be tough and united. He thought it had to get rid of anyone who did not give it full support. He thought it was a successful Party.

Question 3   Sources G and H do agree to a great extent about living conditions in Russia. Source G shows there were blocks of flats and Source H says there were tenements. Source G says the flats were badly built and Source H says exactly the same. Source G says washing facilities were shared by many families and Source H also shows toilets were shared by more than one family. But Source H does say the tenements were centrally heated and Source G does not mention heating at all. Source G suggests the flats were overcrowded but there is no mention of this in Source H.

Investigating

Question 3   Source A is very useful because it is a primary source published at the time of the dock strike and in a newspaper which should be well–informed. It shows how strong the unskilled workers have become.
Source B is also a primary source as it comes from quite close to the events it describes but is part of a book and is not the same type of evidence as Source A. It gives a different view on the strength of the trade unions, showing them as less strong.

Question 4   There is evidence in Source A that unskilled workers were able to form trade unions and were able to win strikes very successfully by the end of the 1880s. The unions were also getting support from public opinion and were getting money from as far away as Australia. Source C shows that some trade unions had very large memberships by 1914 and that they were able to join together to plan strikes.

Source B shows that the trade unions were not always successful. They had made enemies of the middle classes who began to see strikes as a nuisance which should be stopped by the Government. Also the judges and courts did not like trade unions.

Question 5 Some of the evidence in the sources shows trade unions were becoming more successful and growing stronger during the period from the 1880s to the 1920s. Even unskilled workers were able to form unions and win strikes like the dock strike. Also unions such as the miners, the rail workers and transport unions had become very large by 1914 and were able to plan to act together. But there is also evidence that the unions were not popular with the middle classes and the law and that the Government was expected to take action against them. <u>The First World War got in the way of union development but by 1926 they were strong enough to organise a General Strike which was led by the miners</u>. I think unions were stronger in the 1920s than they had been in the 1880s.

> **REMEMBER: You must include something from your own memory in your answer to question 5 to get full marks. In this case, evidence NOT in the sources is underlined.**

Question 6 These two sources do not show fully the attitude to collectivisation. They show only the Communist view. Source F is from a speech by a party official and is biased in favour of collectivisation. It says kulaks who are selfish will never change and will be destroyed. <u>It does not say anything about why they were against collectivisation as they had been forced to give up their grain and animals to feed the towns and many had starved</u>. Source G also shows strong feelings against the kulaks but it is <u>likely the photograph was faked by the Communists to make it seem everyone wanted collectivisation, as they faked other photographs</u>.

OR

Question 7 The sources show typical Communist attitudes towards collectivisation. The Party official is giving the Party view on the kulaks, that they were selfish and would not accept change. In the same way the photograph in Source G is probably faked by the Communists to make it seem all the peasants wanted collectivisation and were against the kulaks. <u>In fact many peasants did not like collectivisation at all because they had seen their food and crops taken away to feed the workers in towns and had seen peasants shot by Communist soldiers if they tried to keep grain for food or to plant next year. Many wanted to keep their own land but were afraid to say so</u>.

> **REMEMBER: You have to use some evidence from your own memory to get full marks for this type of question. In this case evidence not in the sources has been underlined.**

Knowledge and Understanding skills

Introduction

This chapter is split into separate Foundation, General and Credit parts, to make it easier to use. Most of you will find help in two of the three, depending on whether you are preparing to sit the examination at Foundation and General levels or General and Credit levels.

Each part is organised in the same way:
- a short introduction to remind you what you are revising;
- an example of each of the skills;
- questions for you to attempt. (Answers are given at the end of the chapter.)

There are three skills you have to be able to use under the heading Knowledge and Understanding, whether you are attempting Foundation, General or Credit in the examination. You must be able to:
- describe something – like an historical event or person;
- explain something – why it happened or what were its results;
- show why something or someone was or is important.

 ## Foundations/General

At Foundation and General levels you will have sources on the paper to help you.

C Credit level

At Credit level there will be short pieces of information to help you understand what you are to write about. This will usually be a quotation, often only one sentence long.

REMEMBER: At ALL levels it is important to read the questions you are asked carefully AND to look at the number of marks for the question – this will tell you how much evidence you need to give.

You will find answers to all the questions given for you to try, at the end of this section.

F *Foundation level*

At this level you will need to be able to:
- give or complete a simple description of something or someone;
- show why something happened or what its results were;
- show why something or someone was important.

REMEMBER: At this level you write your answers on the examination paper itself.

In the examination paper at Foundation level, questions needing Knowledge and Understanding Skills to answer them are mixed in with Enquiry Skills questions. This means you have two reasons to look carefully at the mark for each question:
- to find out what type of question it is – look at the column that the mark is in on the right hand side of the page;
- to find out how much evidence you need for your answer – usually two or three pieces for 2 or 3 marks.

Here is an example:

Source X is part of a speech by the British Prime Minister at the first meeting of the United Nations.

Source X

Our aim is to stop all war and to create a fair society and a safe world.

Explain why the United Nations was set up?

Reason 1 ....
....

Reason 2 ....
....

You will find at least two reasons in the source which goes before the question.

> **REMEMBER: You can answer a question, like the one on the United Nations above, using information you remember from your course – as long as it is correct. You do not need to use evidence from the source you are given.**

You may even find questions which ask you to fill in missing words in a paragraph. This will also help to tell you what kind of Knowledge and Understanding Skill you should be using. But the clues to the words you need will be in the source you are given to use. Now let's look at the first Knowledge and Understanding Skill.

1   Giving a description

This type of question is easy to recognise. It is usually begins with EITHER

Describe ....
OR
What   ....

Here is an example.
Source A is about the village of Kilmuir on Skye. It was written in 1840.

Source A
The size of the population was rapidly increasing and families had less to live on. Poverty was speedily growing among the people because of falling prices for their produce and unemployment.

Describe changes on Skye around 1840. Mention three things.

1   ....

2   ....

3   ....

All the evidence you need is in Source A. What you have to do is to find it and write it down clearly. Here is what your answer should look like.

1   *The population was growing rapidly.*
2   *People were becoming poorer.*
3   *People were getting less for the things they grew.*

The question could also have been as follows.

What changes happened on Skye around 1840? Mention three changes.

1   The population was growing rapidly.
2   People were becoming poorer.
3   People were getting less for the things they grew.

REMEMBER: Try to answer clearly. This usually means writing a short sentence to make sure the examiner knows that you understand what you are talking about.

Here is an example for you to try:
Source B is about coal mining in the nineteenth century.

Source B
Coal gave off gases when it was exposed by mining. Some were explosive. They were set off by the merest spark, from picking at coal or even dropping a shovel. Floods happened when a hewer broke into an underground lake, but more common was a constant seeping of water into the mine which made life miserable. Even more common was the loss of fingers, crushed by heavy lumps of coal.

*1 Describe **three** dangers facing coal miners during the nineteenth century?*

1 ....

2 ....

3 ....

3 marks

This question could also appear as follows:

Coal miners faced many dangers. There were .... which might .... There was also danger from .... which sometimes rushed in when hewers were digging. There were risks in moving large lumps of coal because fingers might get ....
3 marks

2   The second skill is explaining something

REMEMBER: This type of question can be asked EITHER about why something happened OR about the results of something.

Usually, you will find the question after the source appears like this.

*Why were railway navvies unpopular? Give **two** reasons.*

Because ....

Because. ....

OR

*What were **two** results of the growth of sheep farming in the Highlands?*

1 ....

2 ....

You will need to work out your answer from the source to which the question refers, or you may remember some relevant information from what you have been taught. If you do, then you can write what you remember in place of evidence from the source.

Here is an example for you to study:

Source C is about life in Britain during the Second World War.

Source C

Wartime was difficult for housewives. Nobody starved but food was dull. People were very careful with food. They didn't waste it. Petrol had to come to Britain in ships and was rationed. This meant that there were fewer cars and buses on the road. People used bicycles for short journeys and some hitch-hiked.

*What were **three** results of the war for civilians in Britain?*

1 ....

2 ....

3 ....

1   Food was not very interesting.
2   People were very careful with food.
3   Petrol was rationed.

You could also say that travel became more difficult for people.

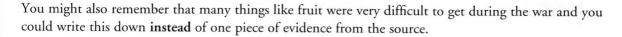

You might also remember that many things like fruit were very difficult to get during the war and you could write this down **instead** of one piece of evidence from the source.

Now here is another example for you to try:

Source D is about young people and support for Hitler and the Nazi Party.

Source D

I was not thinking about Hitler when I saluted but about games, singing and other exciting activities. There was a uniform, a badge, an oath and a salute. There seemed to be nothing to it.

*2   Why did many young people support Hitler and the Nazis? Give **two** reasons.*

Reason ....

Reason ....

3   The third skill is being able to show why something is important

In this type of question you are told that something is **important** and asked to give reasons why this is so. Sometimes a word like 'serious' is used instead of 'important'. The evidence you need is all in the source which goes along with the question. What you have to do is to choose it correctly and write it down clearly.

Here is an example:

Source E describes the introduction of the National Health Service in 1948.

Source E

The 'family doctor' service was, at last, for everyone and they rushed to make use of it. Dentists were soon booked solid for many months ahead. Before long the Health Minister had to make a special appeal to the public to use the National Health Service sensibly. By the end of the first year 187 million prescriptions had been issued and over 8 million dental treatments had been done.

Why was the introduction of the National Health Service so important? Give three reasons.

Because...

Because...

Because...

Because so many people rushed to use it.
Because everyone was now able to go to see a doctor.
Because many people could go to a dentist.

The evidence you need is all in the source. You have to make a judgement about what evidence to use to prove that starting the Health Service was important.

> **REMEMBER: You have to show the examiner you have made a choice of evidence from the source. Not everything in it is relevant and if you just write down large parts of the source you will not get all the marks you need.**

Now here is an example for you to try:

In Source F Winston Churchill describes naval rivalry between Britain and Germany before the first World War.

Source F

What did Germany want this great navy for? Against whom, except us, could she use it? There was a deep and growing feeling that the Germans meant mischief. We realised that Germany would see it as a sign of weakness if we were not willing to build ships.

3   *Why was it important for Britain to build up her navy before the First World War?*
     *Give **two** reasons.*

Reason ....

Reason ....

2 marks

G General level

Most people who sit Foundation level in the final examination will also attempt General level. When you see the examination paper at this level you will notice three big differences from the Foundation level examination paper.

- You do not write your answers on the examination paper but in a separate booklet.
- The question paper has many more pages than the Foundation level paper.
- Each context in the General paper is divided into Section A (Knowledge and Understanding) and Section B (Enquiry Skills).

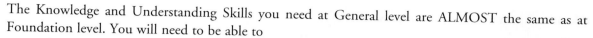

The Knowledge and Understanding Skills you need at General level are ALMOST the same as at Foundation level. You will need to be able to
- describe something – like an historical event or person;
- explain something – what caused it or what were its results;
- make a judgement about the importance of something or someone.

BUT you must look out for these differences from the skills at Foundation level:
- what you write when you are describing something or someone should be longer;
- you will be asked to decide for yourself if something is important or not;
- you will not be told in the question how much evidence to give – you will need to look at the number of marks for the question to help you decide this.

REMEMBER: One of the biggest differences in Knowledge and Understanding answers between Foundation and General is that at GENERAL level you MUST include at least one piece of evidence from your own memory in each answer to get full marks. You will be told this at the start of each Section A – but not in each question!

Now let's look at the skills.

1 Describing someone or something

You will be given one or sometimes two sources to use for this skill. The source(s) will have plenty of evidence for you to choose from so you should read it (them) carefully. Then look at the question AND the number of marks for it, to see how much evidence you need to give.
The question will look like these examples.

Describe some of the changes in mining between 1830 and 1930.	4 marks
What losses did Germany suffer at the end of the First World War?	3 marks
In what ways did the United Nations Organisation plan to maintain world peace?	3 marks

All these questions ask you to write a description, which should be several sentences long and have about three or four pieces of evidence – <u>including at least one from your own memory</u>.

REMEMBER: If the question has four marks and you think you have found four pieces of evidence to use in the source(s), you can use them all BUT you must still add another piece of evidence from your memory to get full marks.

Now here is an example for you to study:
Source A is about life in Russia during the civil war.

Source A
Half its population left Moscow. Petrograd lost almost two-thirds. Nothing came into the country. Nothing went out. Railroad locomotives burned wood. The only thing in ample supply was paper money; by the start of 1919 nearly 34 000 million roubles were in circulation. A year later it was ten times worse. A pack of cigarettes cost a million roubles.

Describe some of the problems facing Russia during the civil war.   4 marks

OR you might be asked:

What problems faced Russia during the civil war?   4 marks

The same answer will fit both questions. Look in the source for evidence of at least three problems, AND remember to think of something you can add to the evidence you find. You answer should look something like this.

During the civil war Russia had several problems. Many people were leaving the cities. Trade with other countries had stopped <u>because of the blockade of Russian ports by the Allies</u>. Money had almost lost its value.

The evidence <u>underlined</u> is not in the source and you need something like this to get full marks.

Here is an example for you to try:
Source B is from a diary kept by Amelia Knight during her journey to the West by wagon train.

Source B
We are creeping along, out of one mud hole and into another all day long. The men and boys are all soaking wet and look sad and uncomfortable. One of the youngsters fell under the wagon but somehow managed to avoid the wheels. Lost one of our oxen: he dropped dead in the yoke.

1 What difficulties faced settlers travelling to the West by wagon train?   4 marks

2   *Explaining the causes or results of something*

Questions on this skill will normally be linked to one source and will look like this:

Explain why the new German government was unpopular after the First World War.   4 marks
OR

Why did people in Russia hate the Tsarina?   4 marks
OR

What were the results of the Russian attempts to build missile sites on Cuba?   3 marks

The source will have plenty of evidence for you to choose from so you should read it carefully. Then look at the question AND the number of marks for it, to see how much evidence you need to give. It is very unlikely the source you are using will say openly what the causes or results are that you are looking for: you will need to work these out from the evidence. But the information you need will be in the source, and often the introduction to the source will help you as well.

> **REMEMBER: If the question has four marks and you think you have found four pieces of evidence to use in the source, you can use them all BUT you must still add another piece of evidence from your memory to get full marks.**

Here is an example for you to study:
Source C describes Lord Kames' efforts to improve his farm land.

Source C

The country was a miserable sight to an improver. There were no sown grasses, no turnip for winter feed; the ground everywhere was overrun with weeds and the tenants were poor and lazy. To encourage his tenants, Lord Kames began by promising money for every improvement they made. But he soon found this to be a mistake.

Why did men like Lord Kames want to improve their farms?   4 marks

As there are four marks for the question you should try to use four pieces of evidence in your answer. Look for three of them from the source and then add a fourth from your memory. Here is what your answer should look like:

Men like Lord Kames wanted to improve their farms because they were not growing the right crops, like turnips for cattle food. Also the fields were full of weeds and the people who lived on his land were poor. If they improved the farms they could make more money from them by growing more crops.

Three pieces of evidence have come from the source and the fourth, which is underlined, has been added from memory to get full marks.

Here are two more examples for you to try:

Source D is about the Ballot Act which introduced secret voting at elections.

Source D

With the secret ballot farmers will be able to return a different set of men to the House of Commons. Until now farmers have had to vote for the landlord's candidate. Therefore, county members of parliament are usually landowners and their supporters. We shall not have honest laws until many landowners are replaced by honest men.

2   What were the results of the introduction of secret voting for Members of Parliament?   3 marks

Source E is about the situation in Russia during the First World War.

Source E
By 1916 the country began to feel a critical food shortage. The causes lay not only in the decline of agricultural production but also in the government's food and supply policy. By forcing all industrial production into the war effort the government deprived villages of their supplies of goods.

3 Why was there discontent in Russia during the First World War? 4 marks

3 *Making a judgement about the importance of something or someone*

This type of question is normally based on one source but can be asked in several ways, for example:

How important was the British blockade in forcing Germany to ask for peace? 3 marks
How serious were the problems facing the government in Russia in September 1917? 4 marks
How successful was the peace treaty signed in Vienna in 1815? 3 marks

In each case you are asked to make a judgement based on evidence in the source AND at least one piece of information from your memory. So it is a good idea always to start your answer by giving your judgement on what the question asks you to consider. You do not have to say, for example, that the 1815 peace treaty was successful. You might think it was only a little successful or that it was not successful at all.
Whatever you decide you must give either three or four pieces of evidence to support your decision, depending on the number of marks for the question. At least one of these must come from your memory, not the source.

Here is an example for you to look at:
Source F is about the new cotton mills in Lochwinnoch.

Source F
Fifty-three new houses have been built and the number, wealth and employment of the inhabitants have been increased within a short time. These rapid increases have been mainly caused by the building of two large cotton mills. One of these mills employs at present 240 people and when the machinery is completed will employ 600.

Was the building of cotton mills important for a town like Lochwinnoch? 4 marks

Yes, building cotton mills was important for towns like Lochwinnoch. The mills meant the towns quickly became richer and more houses were built. They also meant many more jobs for people to do. <u>They also meant other improvements like schools were sometimes made because of the mills.</u>

You must give your judgement – usually in the first sentence as in this answer – but there is no separate mark for this. Marks are given for the evidence you use to support your judgement. In this answer three pieces of evidence come from the source and one is from memory, which is underlined.

Now here is an example for you to try:

Source G is about the use of gas during the First World War.

Source G

Gas was soon in use by all the armies. It appeared as a greenish-yellow cloud which gradually changed into a bluish-white mist, drifting with the wind towards the trenches. Here it created utter terror – no one knew what to do. It is said some young officers advised their men to urinate into their handkerchiefs and hold them to their noses. Not surprisingly it did not work. Soon gas masks were distributed to the troops on both sides.

4   *How successful was the use of gas as a weapon in the First World War?*   4 marks

Credit level

The Knowledge and Understanding Skills you need are the same as at General level, that is you must be able to
- describe something – like an historical event or person;
- explain something – what caused it or what were its results;
- make a judgement about the importance of something or someone.

However, there are two differences you should notice between the examination at General and Credit level.
- The examination paper still has a Section A for Knowledge and Understanding BUT there are NO sources for you to use in this section.
- ONE of the Section A answers in ONE unit will ask you to write a short essay.

This means that for ALL your answers to Knowledge and Understanding questions at Credit level, you will have to use only evidence from your own memory. Every question in Section A will have a short introduction, which is meant to help you think about what the question is asking, but it will not contain any evidence you can use in your answer. Here are some examples of questions.

Nazis gloried in being racist.

Describe the racial policies of the National Socialist government between 1934 and 1939.   5 marks

OR

A steam driven mule needed only one operator to control 100 spindles.

Explain the importance of new machinery to the growth of the textile industry before 1850.   4 marks

These short introductions are to help you to see what the question is about. There is no evidence in them for you to use in your answer.

> **REMEMBER: One Section A question in one Unit will ask you to write a short essay of several paragraphs, so look out for this. The number of marks will be more than for any other question.**

Here are some examples using each of the Knowledge and Understanding Skills.

1 Describing something or someone

This kind of question will usually start with words like:
- Describe . . .
- Give an account of . . .
- What . . .BE CAREFUL – some questions which start with *What* go on to ask about causes, results or importance.

You are expected to just write a clear description in answer to such questions – so if you find yourself writing a lot about **why** something happened you are using the wrong skill.
Look at the number of marks for the question. This will tell you how much evidence you need to use. Here is an example:

Support for farming improvements came from the landowners and wealthier tenant farmers.

Describe some of the improvements in farming between 1750 and 1850.   5 marks

Your answer should just be a description of either four or five improvements depending on how much evidence you use in each. DO NOT try to say why they happened or how important they were.

There were many improvements. New crops like potatoes were brought more into use on farms in the Lowlands.[1] Farmers began to try ways of getting better crops by using a system called rotation.[2] Under this system the crop grown in a field was changed regularly so that the field did not get worn out.[3] Also many landowners began to enclose their land making fields bigger and better.[4] Some farmers used new and better ploughs.[5]

This answer mentions four improvements and extends one of them – about crop rotation – which also gets a mark.

REMEMBER: You can probably get up to two marks for giving additional information about something – in this case crop rotation or enclosures or new style ploughs.

Now here is an example for you to try:

The world's first complete railway for goods traffic and passengers was the Liverpool and Manchester railway.

1   *What changes took place in the transportation of goods and passengers between 1830 and 1900?*

5 marks

2   *Explaining the causes or results of something*

This type of question will usually begin with words like:
- Why did . . .
- Explain why . . .
- Explain the reasons for . . .
- Explain the effects of . . .
- What were the results of . . .

Read the question carefully to make sure there is not a word like 'important' or 'serious' in it – because that makes it the third skill not this one – and to find how many marks it has, so that you know how much evidence to use in your answer.

Here are some examples:

In August 1945 the US decided to drop an atomic bomb on a Japanese city.

What were the consequences of the dropping of atomic bombs on Hiroshima and Nagasaki?   4 marks

Output of coal rose rapidly. In 1830 output was about 30 million tons per year. By 1880 it was over 150 million tons.

Why was there an increased demand for coal between 1830 and 1880?   4 marks

REMEMBER: You are explaining the causes or results of something, so you should be making a lot of use of words like 'because' or 'as' to avoid just giving a description.

Here is an example to look at:
> There had been many wars in the history of the world, but none had the impact of the Great War.

> *Why did the First World War cause people to react so strongly?*   5 marks

Your answer should give four or five reasons, depending on how you use your evidence – <u>and must not just list results of the First World War</u>.

> *People reacted very strongly after the First World War mainly because of the large number of casualties suffered by the countries involved.[1] Germany lost over 2 million men and Russia nearly as many.[2] Also many of the men who survived the war were very badly affected by the horrors of the trenches and hated war.[3] For example many were blinded by gas and could not work. [4] The countries involved had spent large amounts of money fighting the war and so faced great financial difficulties and wanted to make sure this never happened again.[5]*

The first sentence makes it clear you understand what skill your are being asked to use. Then there are two pieces of evidence about the effect of casualties and two about the horrors of war. The final evidence is about the effect of the great financial cost of the war.

Now here is an example for you to try:
> What Germans were looking for in Hitler and the Nazis was, in fact, not a solution but a salvation.

> *2 Why did Germans support Hitler and the Nazis in the 1930s?*   4 marks

3   *Making a judgement about the importance of something*

This type of question is usually quite easy to recognise, because it often contains words like 'importance' or 'serious'. For example:

> *How important was the development of the tank for the outcome of the war on the Western Front?*
>   4 marks
> *Were the events at Amritsar important?*   4 marks
> *How serious was slavery as an issue between North and South in 1860?*   5 marks

Here is an example to study:
> The motor car was developed in the 1880s but its cost made it a plaything of the rich.

> *How important was the development of road transport in the twentieth century?*   4 marks

> **REMEMBER: The question ask you to make a judgement. It is up to you to decide what that judgement should be – Important? Not Important? Quite important? But you must offer evidence to support your choice and the number of marks tells you how much to use.**

The growth of road transport in the twentieth century was very important for several reasons. At first cars were very expensive but after the First World War new techniques of mass production made them cheaper, and more people could afford them so the numbers on the roads grew quickly.[1] This meant new jobs making cars and things for cars which meant new industries. [2] The growth of road transport also meant goods and people could be delivered to more places more quickly and cheaply.[3] But more cars in towns began to cause problems with traffic jams and pollution and accidents so it was not all a good thing.[4]

It is a good idea to give your judgement at the start as this makes it clear to the examiner that you understand what you should be doing. In this answer three good points about road transport are balanced by one problem it has caused, to give an overall balance to your judgement.

You can also give balance to an answer by arguing that one piece of evidence is more important than any others – for example, in the answer above, that better delivery service was the most important development in road transport because it helped people move away from overcrowded town centres.

Here is an example for you to try:

The most dangerous crisis occurred in 1962.

3   *How serious a threat to world peace was the Cuban Missile Crisis?*   4 marks

Writing a short essay at Credit level

This is an important part of the Knowledge and Understanding Skills section of you examination. The short essay question carries more marks than any other question – 8 marks in the present examination. It can make the difference between a Grade 1 and a Grade 2, or between a pass and a fail at Credit level. The essay question can come in any of the three Knowledge and Understanding Skills. You can easily recognise it because it will:

- say you need to write a short essay e.g.
  (Note: for this answer you should write a short essay of serveral paragraphs);

- give you a choice of things to write about;
- have an unusually high number of marks.

To be successful in the essay question you need to
- answer on the topic asked about in the question;
- use the right Knowledge and Understanding Skill;
- use between three and six pieces of relevant evidence;
- write clearly and in paragraphs.

Here is an example of what an essay question looks like:

The Scotsman newspaper was founded in 1817 to increase support for peaceful reform. (Note: for this answer you should write a short essay of several paragraphs.)

Explain why there were demands between 1750 and 1850 for
EITHER

    (a) Parliamentary reform;   8 marks

OR

    (b) improvements in public health.   8 marks

Let's take a look at what is required in a short essay in each of the three skills.
You need about six pieces of evidence to get full marks but this can be
- six separate pieces
- three separate pieces BUT with each one having extra information added on – as you saw in the sample answers given earlier in this section.

To help you, points of evidence are numbered in the outlined answers which follow.

1   *Describing something*

This is probably the simplest of the essay answers to write. You need to provide more evidence than you gave in the 4 or 5 mark answer, and you should think about how to organise it to make it as clear as possible.
It will help to make your answer clearer if you set it out in at least three paragraphs. For instance, if you were asked to write a short essay in answer to the following:

Describe working conditions in coal mines between 1830 and 1914.   8 marks

you could organise your answer as follows.

Paragraph 1 *Mention the bad conditions in mines around 1830. Women and children did heavy work underground, women carried coal from coal face up ladders to the* surface.(1) Very young children did jobs such as opening and closing trap doors.(2) Dangers from things like roof falls and gas.(3)

Paragraph 2 1842 Mines Act improved working conditions by stopping women and young children from working underground.(4) The Mines Acts in 1850 and 1860 increased the age for underground working from 10 to 12.(5)

Paragraph 3 New techniques and machines used in mines and this made them safer, for example, new ways of blasting coal out, use of electricity to light mines.(6)

REMEMBER: Practise writing this kind of short essay answer so that you can do it quickly and without making it just a list of facts.

2   Explaining the causes or results of something

This type of answer can also be successfully written in the three paragraph format, for example in answer to the question:-

Why did the standard of public health improve between 1850 and 1914?   8 marks

Paragraph 1 There was a great improvement in public health 1850–1950. Effects of acts like the Public Health Act 1848 beginning to spread.(1) This allowed local authorities to improve water supplies and waste disposal.(2) This work was continued and improved on by Sir John Simon who was responsible for the 1875 Public Health Act which strengthened all the public health legislation.(3)

Paragraph 2 Improvement also due to better food supplies partly due to better transportation but also to acts like the Food and Drugs Act, 1875.(4) Medical advances also helped make people healthier, for example, more people were vaccinated against smallpox.(5)

Paragraph 3 Although there were great improvements there were still many problems often due to bad housing for example in Scottish towns, where slums continued till after First World War.(6)

The third paragraph not only adds to the evidence provided but also balances the answer by showing awareness of the continued existence of serious health problems beyond the end of the period in the question.

3   Making a judgement about the importance of something

Again, you can use the three paragraph format. In the case of this type of question it is essential to give your judgement clearly, either in paragraph 1 or in paragraph 3 – or in both! Here is an example:

Was the assassination of Archduke Franz Ferdinand and his wife the most important reason why the First World War began?   8 marks

Paragraph 1 *Disagree. The assassination was the reason war broke out in 1914 rather than later but not the main reason for the war.(1) Long term major disagreements and rivalry between Serbia and Austria over the Balkans.(2) Russia was involved as an ally to Serbia and Germany as an ally to Austria.(3)*

Paragraph 2 *War was due to the existence of two major, rival armed camps in Europe, with Britain, France and Russia on one side and Germany, Austria and Italy on the other.(4) Germany feared attack on two sides and had a war plan which called for swift action if war threatened.(5)*

Paragraph 3 *Britain and Germany had become serious rivals in a naval arms race because Britain distrusted German reasons for building dreadnoughts and this made war likely.(6) For all these reasons most European countries expected war to happen sometime.*

The comment about the assassination, as the immediate cause of war but not the most important, gives balance to the answer. You could also provide balance by expanding your evidence about the two armed camps, suggesting that this was the main reason for the war.

Answers to sample questions

This is the kind of evidence you should be giving.

Foundation Level

Question 1   There was gas that exploded.
There were floods.
Fingers got crushed by rocks.
gases   explode   water   crushed

Question 2   because they got to have fun
because they wore uniforms/badges

Question 3   Reason 1 to be able to fight Germany
Reason 2 so that Germany would not think Britain was weak.

General level

Evidence not in the sources is underlined.

Question 1   The journey was very slow.(1) The roads were bad and travel was very uncomfortable.(2) People could be injured by the wagons.(3) <u>There was danger of Indian attacks.</u>(4)

Question 2   Because of secret voting a different kind of MP was elected by farmers.(1) It meant they could now choose their own MP and not just the one their landlord wanted.(2) It also meant that <u>the amount of bribery and corruption at elections was reduced</u>.(3)

Question 3   There was discontent because food was very short.(1) People were angry at the government because of the way it dealt with food shortages.(2) They were discontented because they did not have things they needed because the government put everything into fighting the war.(3) <u>The soldiers were unhappy because they did not have enough weapons to fight with</u>.(4)

Question 4   Gas was only quite successful as a weapon. At first it made soldiers very frightened as they did not know what to do about it.(1) The first gas masks men used did not work.(2) But it depended on the wind to reach the enemy and this could change.(3) <u>Also there were sometimes problems in releasing the gas because the cylinders could not be opened.</u>(4)

C   *Credit level*

> **REMEMBER: The following answers give an example of the kind of evidence you can use. There is likely to be other relevant evidence you have learned during your course and you can use this equally well.**

Question 1   In 1830 canals still carried a lot of goods and passengers.(1) Also many people travelled by coach and goods went in wagons.(2) But the number of railways grew very quickly after the 1840s (3) and goods and passengers could travel much more quickly by rail.(4) By 1900 road transport began to become popular again as the motor car began to take over from horse power on the roads.(5)

Question 2   Germans supported Hitler for several reasons. Germany had suffered serious economic collapse during the 1920s because of inflation.(1) Many middle and upper class people as well as the poor had lost all their wealth when money lost its value and they had to sell their goods to live and they all blamed the Weimar government for this.(2) Hitler also won support because he promised to overturn the Treaty of Versailles and give Germany back her place in the world.(3) Many middle and upper class Germans supported him because he opposed communism which seemed to threaten them with revolution.(4)

Question 3   The Cuban missile crisis was a very serious threat to world peace. Tension had been building up between Russia and America since the end of the Second World War.(1) The Cold War had split the world into two rival camps led by America and Russia who both had atomic weapons.(2) Both the leaders of America and Russia were very strong-willed men who would not want to back down in a crisis.(3) The Americans actually sent out ships to stop and search all ships suspected of bringing missiles to Cuba and had the Russians not backed down then a World War could have begun.(4)

Using visual sources

Introduction

Visual sources which can appear in the examination papers may be:
- paintings or drawings
- photographs
- cartoons
- diagrams
- maps
- posters
- tables

At ALL levels in the examination you will find a few examples of visual sources used. Some people like this kind of source evidence because it is different, or because they feel it is easier to use. At Credit level visual sources only appear in Section B: Enquiry Skills.

Normally you will find that pictures or maps appear more in contexts that deal with the eighteenth or nineteenth centuries, and photographs are usually from the twentieth century. Posters and tables may appear in any context.

Wherever they appear you will always be given some information about them, for example you may be told:

- who produced them;
- when they were produced;
- what they say or show.

All sources, written or visual, are there to help you. Therefore, the information they contain will be clearly visible – so if you know what kind of evidence to look for you should find it easily.

In the case of drawings, photographs, cartoons and posters there are three things you can always start by asking about the source.

1 When was it produced?
2 Who produced it?
3 What does it show?

If you can answer some or all of these questions you will be well on the way to being able to use the source successfully in answer to most questions.

Using Drawings

Source A is a drawing of Glasgow about 1760.

Source A

Source B is a drawing of Glasgow about 1850.

Source B

Foundation level

At Foundation level you could be asked questions about ONE of these drawings, probably the second one. For example:

1   Describe Glasgow in 1835. Mention two things.   2 marks

Glasgow was . . . *full of factories.*
Glasgow was . . . *a very dirty town.*

2   Look at Source B. Why was Glasgow not a nice place to live in 1835? 2 marks

Because . . . *it was full of smoking factories.*
Because . . . *it looks a very crowded city.*

3   Why is Source B good evidence about Glasgow in the early eighteenth century?   2 marks

Because . . . *it is a primary source.*
Because . . . *it shows you what it looked like.*

General level

At General level you could be given Source B and asked to do things like:

1   Describe an industrial town in the 1830s.   3 marks

Industrial towns were full of factories giving out smoke(1) Factories were often very close together(2) <u>and houses were built next to the factories because they were often built by factory owners for their workers</u>.(3)

The evidence <u>underlined</u> is from memory because you need this kind of evidence at General level. You might find Source B in the Enquiry Skills section with a question such as:

2   Is Source B valuable as evidence about industrial towns in the 1830s? Give reasons for your answer.
   3 marks

Yes it is valuable because it is a primary source from the middle of the 1830s.(1) It shows clearly what factories did to a town like Glasgow.(2) Because it is a drawing the artist might have exaggerated it to make things seem worse than they were.(3)

Or you might even find Sources A and B in the Enquiry Skills section with a question such as:

3   Compare the evidence about Glasgow in Sources A and B.   3 marks

Source A shows Glasgow as a city with few industries and B shows a very industrial city.(1) Source A shows an unpolluted city and B shows a city covered in smoke from the factories.(2) Source A shows a small city and B shows what a much larger city Glasgow has become. (3)

Credit level

At Credit level you would only find Sources A and B in the Enquiry Skills section of the examination paper. A question could be:

1   How valuable is Source B as evidence about the effects of industrialisation on cities in Scotland?   4 marks

Quite valuable, because it might be a primary source but it is not clear if it was drawn in 1835 or later.(1) It does show the effects of industrialisation like pollution clearly (2) but we do not know for what purpose the artist drew it in this way.(3) As it only shows Glasgow it is not possible to say all cities were affected by industrialisation in the same way.(4)

Using Photographs

Photographs are easier to work with than drawings. They usually show you what was actually there at a particular moment in time.

Knowledge and Understanding

If you find them as a source for a Knowledge and Understanding question you can be certain you do not have to worry about how accurate they are. Simply look at what they show you because it is likely you will just be asked to describe what you see, for example:

Source A is a photograph of a British trench in the First World War.

Source A

 Foundation level

Describe a First World War trench. Mention two things about it.

1 ....

2 ....

 General level

Describe conditions in a First World War trench. 3 marks

Enquiry Skills

If Source A was followed by an Enquiry Skills question you should think about the fact that you do not have a definite date for the photograph and the possibility that the photographer picked this trench because it was dry and quite well constructed. The questions could be:

Foundation level

Why is Source A valuable as evidence about trenches in the First World War?

Reason ....
....
Reason ....
....

General level

How useful is Source A as evidence about First World War trenches? 3 marks

Credit level

To what extent does Source A accurately show what a First World War trench was like? You should use your own knowledge and give reasons for your answer. 4 marks

Using Posters and Cartoons

Both posters and cartoons are produced in order to directly influence what you are thinking. Therefore, the posters and cartoons you may see in the examination will always have an obvious purpose in mind. You will almost always be told things about the posters and cartoons that are used, such as,

- when they were produced;
- who produced them;
- what they say or show – if the print is small or they are in a foreign language;
- who is shown in a cartoon – if it is not very obvious.

This kind of information will allow you to answer most of the questions you are likely to be asked.

Source A

▲ *Propaganda posters from the 1932 Nazi election campaign. The posters on the left promise freedom for children and those on the right promise work and bread.*

Knowledge and Understanding

At Foundation and General levels you may occasionally find Knowledge and Understanding questions based on posters – but hardly ever on cartoons. For example, look at the posters in Source A:

 ## Foundation level

What two things did the Nazis promise Germans?

 ## General level

Why did Germans vote for the Nazis?

 ## Credit level

How important was propaganda to the success of the Nazis?

Enquiry Skills

At all levels you are even more likely to find posters and cartoons linked to Enquiry Skills questions. Source A could be followed by questions like:

Foundation level

Why is Source A valuable evidence about the Nazi Party? Give two reasons.

General level

Is Source A useful evidence about the Rise of the Nazi Party?

3 marks

Credit level

Is Source A typical of propaganda used by the Nazi Party?

4 marks

Cartoons linked to Enquiry skills questions always come with a lot of information, like when they were drawn and who they show. You can usually decide quite easily who in a cartoon is meant to be good, and who is meant to be bad. Look at Source B for instance, there is no doubt about who is good and who is bad. Source B was published in *Punch* in August 1914. The man is meant to be Germany and the little boy is Belgium.

Source B

NO THOROUGHFARE

BRAVO, BELGIUM!

Foundation level

Give two reasons why Source B is useful as evidence about British opinions on Germany in 1914?

General level

Is Source B valuable evidence of the British attitude to Germany in 1914? 3 marks

Credit level

How valuable is Source B as evidence about British attitudes to Germany in 1914? 4 marks

Some Do's and Don'ts

Some Do's – before the examination

- Keep your notes and handouts up to date during your course – having to sort out a pile of papers in the weeks before the examination is a waste of your valuable time.
- Try to start revising about four weeks before the examination.
- Revise by making yourself comfortable and reading through your notes etc. context by context.
- Look at past examination papers or text books if you can, and practice recognising different types of questions and planning answers – perhaps with someone else who is taking the examination.
- Some people find it helpful to write out short notes with the main points from the topics they have studied, as a way of memorising information.
- Practise making plans on different topics for the essay question and perhaps write out some of them – you should only allow yourself about 12 minutes for a short essay.

Some Do's – during the examination

- Make sure you answer on the contexts you have studied.
- Read sources, questions and marks carefully, so that you know what you are being asked to do and how much evidence to use.
- Check you have answered every question in the contexts you pick, especially if you leave one out to go back to later!
- If a question asks 'Why …' something happened, make sure you use a word like 'because' in your first sentence to help organise your answer, and to show the examiner you know what you should be doing.

- If the question asks you for a judgement, for example of 'importance', it is a good idea to give your judgement in the first sentence. Read over your answer to make sure you have not changed your mind half way through!
- Remember you can always use information from your memory and will get marks for it – if it is correct and relevant!
- Take a watch into the examination and make sure you do not take too long on the first two contexts on which you answer. You have only one hour at Foundation level, one and a half hours at General level, one and three quarter hours at Credit level.

And two Don'ts

Avoid over-working the night before the examination. Anything extra you learn is likely to be balanced by things you miss in the examination through being tired.

For Foundation and General levels, there is no need to try to memorise loads of facts. The sources and the questions should jog your memory, if you have studied the contexts carefully and revised them in the weeks before the examination.

Unit I

Glossary

Chartists   People who supported the Six Points of Charter of 1836 – such as votes for all men over 21 and payment for MPs. Most of their ideas are now accepted.

Cholera   Deadly disease spread mainly through contaminated water. Appeared in Britain in 1831 and killed thousands, especially in the towns. Appeared again 1848 and 1861 and helped the demand for improved water in towns.

Clearances   During the late eighteenth and early nineteenth centuries many crofters in the Highlands were evicted to make way for sheep farming. Some evictions were very violent. Many crofters moved to Central Scotland or abroad.

Corn Laws   Introduced in 1815 to protect British farmers from foreign competition when corn prices rose in this country. Meant bread prices stayed high and the poor suffered.

Cottage industry   In the eighteenth century, work such as spinning and weaving was done in the home by hand or on small machines. Sometimes called 'domestic' industry.

Democracy   A form of government in which all adults share in some way in the running of the country (e.g. by having a vote).

Depression   A time of economic hardship when businesses lose money and close and many people are unemployed.

Enclosure   Landowners brought small fields together to make bigger fields, surrounded by hedges/walls, and introduced other farming improvements. Farm labourers and many tenant-farmers suffered as they lost their jobs.

Factory 1750–1850 mainly textile work (cotton) moved into large buildings called (manu)factories, where bigger machines powered by water or steam produced much more than workers in domestic industry could.

Franchise The limits which show who has the right to vote.

Improvers Landowners in the eighteenth and nineteenth centuries began to look for ways to improve their farms, e.g. by enclosing fields, crop rotation, using mechanical fertilisers, new machines.

Inflation When money loses its value and prices rise – sometimes very quickly!

Labour Party Formed in 1906 out of several organisations which had appeared in the 1890s. Meant to represent the needs of working people.

Mass production A form of manufacturing large quantities of goods, e.g. cars, which has grown in the twentieth century, and is often based on a moving production line along which workers add parts to help make the product. Often workers repeat the same task over and over all day.

NHS National Health Service – set up in 1948 to give free medical treatments to everyone, not just those with money.

Owen, Robert Manager of the New Lanark cotton mill from 1800. The factory became a model of good practice because of the care Owen took of his workers and their children.

Penicillin Antibiotic discovered by Alexander Fleming in 1928. Developed during the Second World War and has saved millions of lives.

Radical A supporter of rapid extensive reform – e.g. in the way a country is run.

Rotation (crop) Changing what is grown in a field from year to year to help keep the soil fertile.

Suffragettes Supporters of the campaign for women's rights – especially the right to vote – in the years from 1880 to 1914. Finally turned to the use of violence against government property when other means failed.

Suffragists Also wanted improved rights for women but preferred to use legal means to make their case.

Turnpike Turnpike roads were ones on which tolls were charged to pay for their upkeep. Road engineers like John Macadam and Thomas Telford were employed to improve surfaces and bridges on some of these roads.

Vaccination A way of making people immune to some diseases by giving a minor dose of the disease or a related disease to make them resistant to diseases such as smallpox (discovered by Edward Jenner in 1798).

Wall Street Crash 1929. Share prices on the American stock market fell very quickly and many people and businesses were ruined. Effects felt all round the world.

Time Line
POPULATION/HEALTH

1750	Scottish population estimated as 1.25 million. British population estimated as 5.5 million. Only 20 percent of people lived in towns.
1796	Edward Jenner discovered vaccination against smallpox.
1801	First official census of British population. Repeated every ten years since.
1832	First cholera epidemic in Britain. Thousands died, especially in towns.
1834	Poor Law Amendment Act forced the poor who wanted help to enter the Poorhouse where conditions were very harsh.
1842	Edwin Chadwick produced his report on living conditions in towns. It made clear the need for better water supplies and sanitation to stop disease.
1845	Poor Law Act (Scotland) similar to earlier British Act, but made it easier for the old and the sick to get help outside the Poorhouse.
1847	Chloroform discovered by James Simpson. More people survived operations.
1851	Scottish population now 2.88 million. British population 20.8 million. Over 50 percent now lived in towns.
1875	Food and Drugs Act improved health by making things people consumed purer.
1875	Public Health Act tidied up laws on health especially water supply and sanitation.
1875	Artisans' Dwellings Act gave local councils powers to clear slums.
1906–09	Liberal Government brought in several laws to protect the young and the elderly – providing free school meals and medical examinations for children and pensioners.
1909	Housing Act forced local councils to rehouse at least 50 percent of families when slums were cleared.
1911	Liberal Government set up National Insurance scheme to help workers who became ill and the following year also provided help for the unemployed.
1920	Welwyn Garden City begun and idea of 'new towns' to help clear slums started. In Scotland 'new towns' began to appear after 1945 – e.g. Irvine in 1947.
1924	Wheatley Housing Act gave money to local councils to help pay for new housing to replace slums.
1941	Penicillin used in human trials.
1946–48	Labour Government improved National Insurance and set up National Health Service on the basis of the Beveridge Report. Provided free medical services for all.
1951	Scottish population now 4.9 million. British population 49 million. Great majority lived in towns.
1974	National Health Service reorganised to put hospitals and other medical services under district health authorities.

Time Line
FARMING 1750–1920

1750–1800	Major farming improvements such as: • better animal breeding; • crop rotation; • enclosures of fields; • better machines for ploughing, threshing etc.
1815	End of wars against France. Corn Law passed to protect farmers from foreign competition.
1816	Trial of Patrick Sellar over deaths of crofters during clearance of tenants in Sutherland.
1820s	Bell's mechanical reaper improved the cutting of cereal crops. Meant fewer jobs for labourers.
1840s	More improvements in farming – clay pipes to improve drainage and new chemical fertilisers.
1845	Famine in Ireland due to failure of potato crop. Many emigrated to Britain or America.
1846	Corn Laws repealed. Britain became free trade country.
1850s–70s	British farming very successful, because of improvements and further changes, such as use of steam powered machines.
1875	Start of depression in farming due to cheap imports from abroad and poor harvests at home.
1900–18	Recovery in farming because many farmers took advantage of the growing market for fruit and vegetables.

Time Line
INDUSTRY 1750–1980

1759	Carron iron works set up near Falkirk.
1760s	Important inventions in textile making – such as James Hargreaves' 'Jenny' and Richard Arkwright's water frame, both of which made spinning much faster.
1779	Samuel Crompton combined the jenny and the water frame in his 'mule' and added steam power.
1781	James Watt invented a gearing system which allowed a steam engine to drive a wheel.
1786	David Dale built a cotton mill at New Lanark. The factory was taken over 14 years later by Robert Owen and became a model of good factory conditions.
1812	'Comet' provided the first steam powered passenger service on the Clyde.
1815	Humphrey Davy invented the 'safety lamp' which helped prevent explosions in mines.
1825	Stockton to Darlington railway opened.
1830	Liverpool to Manchester railway opened. Built by George Stephenson. Railways beginning to provide serious competition for turnpike roads and canals.
1833	Factory Act. Tried to limit hours worked in factories by young people.
1842	Mines Act. Stopped women and children working underground in mines.
1844	Railway Act. Made railways more reliable and cheaper. Followed by a period of very rapid growth in railways.
1850s	Iron ships with steam engines began to replace wooden sailing ships. Clyde became a major centre for ship building.
1860s	Wooden sailing ships called 'Clippers' still built on Clyde and in Aberdeen as they were better than steam ships on longer routes.
1860s	Steam power used in mines to haul coal, gradually replacing pit ponies.
1871	Trade Unions made legal.
1875	Trade Unions allowed to organise peaceful picketing.
1888	Match Girls at Bryant & May won their strike against their employer, with much popular support.
1889	Dockers' Strike showed unskilled workers could organise a union and win a strike.
1890s	Electricity used in some mines and in towns to power trams.
1900–14	Ship building industry very successful – one fifth of all ships were made in Scotland.
1913	William Morris opened a car works in Oxford, copying 'mass production' methods of Ford in America.
1920–40	Ship building in decline because of loss of trade after the First World War.
1926	General Strike. Led by miners but unable in the end to win concessions from employers and government.

1930s	Expansion of roads and tourism in Scotland. Traffic lights in towns. Road transport becoming serious threat to railways.
1934	Driving test introduced.
1945	End of the Second World War. Ship building went into serious decline because of foreign competition and failure to modernise.
1947	Railways nationalised by Labour government.
1959	M1 motorway opened.
1960s	First motorways built in Scotland.
1964	Beeching Report caused closure of main railway lines and loss of 50 percent of staff.
1981	65 percent of families in Scotland have a car. Many towns suffering from traffic jams and pollution.

Time Line
GOVERNMENT 1750–1980

1761	In Scotland as in the rest of Britain voting was limited to men with wealth and property. Many towns had no MPs.
1789	Revolution in France. Monarchy overthrown and a republic was set up. Many people in Britain showed support for French ideas.
1815	Monarchy restored in France.
1819	'Peterloo' Massacre. Troops killed several members of a crowd at a reform meeting in Manchester. Government passed laws making such meetings illegal.
1820	Radical Wars in Scotland. Political unrest in central Scotland, especially in Glasgow. Fighting between troops and reformers at Bonnymuir, near Falkirk.
1832	Parliamentary Reform Act. Increased number of voters slightly. Still only men with property and wealth could vote. Some growing towns got MPs.
1836	Chartist Movement began. It wanted more reforms, including vote for all men over 21, payment for MPs.
1848	Year of Revolutions. Great unrest across Europe. Little trouble in Britain.
1867	Second Parliamentary Reform Act. Big increase in number of men who could vote. Franchise still linked to wealth and property.
1872	Ballot Act made voting secret and greatly reduced corruption at elections.
1884	Third Parliamentary Reform Act allowed two out of every three men to vote.
1903	Women's Social and Political Union set up led by Mrs Emmeline Pankhurst to win votes for women.
1906	Labour Party created to represent ordinary working people.
1911	Liberal Party reforms of parliament – limited power of the House of Lords, MPs to be paid, parliament to sit for five years maximum.
1912	Suffragettes began a campaign of violence against government property to win the vote for women.
1913	The suffragette Emily Davison, was killed by the King's horse as she was trying to interrupt the Derby.
1914	Suffragettes stopped all actions when war began. This, and the war work they did, gained much support for their cause after the war.
1918	Parliamentary Reform Act gave the vote to men over 21 and women over 30.
1924	First Labour Government.
1928	Women over 21 allowed to vote.
1934	Scottish National Party established.

| 1945 | Third Labour Government introduced many social reforms, such as the National Health Service. |
| 1979 | Referendum on a separate assembly to govern Scotland. Narrow majority voted 'yes' but not enough to get the assembly. |

Unit II

Glossary
The First World War

Armistice   A cease fire either temporary – as at Christmas 1914 – or permanent as in 1918.

Armed Camps   The division of Europe before 1914 into two rival groups each arming itself for war.

Arms Race   Usually refers to rivalry between Britain and Germany over naval strength, especially in relation to the number of new battleships (dreadnoughts) each had.

Black Hand   Serbian secret society held responsible by Austria for assassination of Archduke Franz Ferdinand in Sarajevo, 1914.

Disarmament   The attempt by the Allies to prevent future wars by greatly reducing the arms countries could hold – especially Germany.

Dreadnought   1906 new style battleship launched by Britain. Much bigger, faster and more heavily armed than any other warship.

Gas   First used 1915 by Germans on the Russian front, then by all sides. Initially chlorine or phosgene gases used, then tear gases and later mustard gas which was the most feared.

Home front   The First World War was a total war, in that everyone was affected or involved in some way. Government used propaganda to encourage civilians to help the war effort at home, e.g. by not wasting food.

Machine gun   Rapid fire automatic weapon which made old style infantry and cavalry attacks impossible.

Mobilisation   Ordering army to 'action stations'.

No Man's Land   The land between the two opposing front line trenches. Often filled with barbed wire, mines and holes caused by shells.

Reparations   Money to be paid (£6000 million by Germany) to the victors to help make up for the cost of war.

Sanctions   Steps taken to try to force a country to agree to or stop certain actions. Usually involve cutting off or restricting trade with the country.

Schlieffen Plan   German plan to march through Belgium and defeat France in less than two months in the event of war, so that she could then turn to fight the Russians, who were expected to be slower to mobilise.

Tank   Tracked armoured vehicle developed by Britain (by the navy because the army turned the idea down!) and France to be able to attack across almost any ground and overcome the problems caused by machine guns and deep trenches, thereby breaking the stalemate on the Western Front.

Trench war   System of defence relying on a series of deep ditches forming a front line, supply lines and reserve lines.

Triple Entente   France, Britain and Russia. They agreed to cooperate if attacked by Germany or her allies.

Triple Alliance   Germany, Austria–Hungary and Italy agreed to fight together if any one of them was attacked.

Ultimatum   Terms which have to be accepted under threat.

War Guilt   One of the peace terms forced on Germany was that she accept the blame for starting the First World War and for the terrible loss of life and damage it caused.

Time Line
COOPERATION AND
CONFLICT 1890–1930

1882	Triple Alliance of Germany, Austria–Hungary and Italy formed.
1890	Kaiser Wilhelm II decides Germany needs colonies – 'a place in the sun'.
1891	Germany decides not to renew her alliance with Russia – preferring her alliance with Austria and Italy.
1892	France and Russia form an alliance for defence against Germany.
1898	Britain insists she prefers 'splendid isolation' from Europe.
1899–1902	Boer War showed up weaknesses in British army and the Kaiser encouraged the Boers.
1904	Britain and France reached an 'understanding' (Entente Cordiale) over their colonial disputes in North Africa.
1905	Russia badly defeated in war against Japan.
1905	J R Haldane organises reforms in British army e.g. Territorial Army set up and a rapid response force – the British Expeditionary Force (BEF) – was established. Germany High Command adopts the Schlieffen Plan which requires the German army to attack France through Belgium in the event of war, avoiding defences along the French border.
1905 & 1911	Two crises over Morocco caused disputes between France and Germany (and involved Britain).
1906	Britain launched HMS *Dreadnought* as part of strengthening her navy.
1907	The Entente between Britain and France is extended to include Russia and becomes the Triple Entente. Britain still not committed to fight for France or Russia.
1908	Austria seized Bosnia, Herzegovina and angered Serbia and Russia who were however persuaded not to go to war on this occasion.
1912	Britain and France agreed to split naval responsibilities – with France concentrating on the Mediterranean and Britain the North Sea. Britain formed Royal Flying Corps, the start of the Royal Air Force.
1912	First Balkan War: Turkey defeated by the Balkan League (Serbia, Bulgaria, Greece) and both Austria and Russia mobilised their armies. Danger of major European war.
1913	Second Balkan War: members of Balkan League fought amongst themselves. Serbia gained most and felt able to stand up to Austria. Germany promised to help Austria, if needed.
1914	June/July: a Serb, Gavrilo Princip, assassinated Archduke Franz Ferdinand of Austria and his wife. Austria blamed Serbia and gave her an impossible ultimatum. Serbia tried to avoid war but Austria was determined to fight and declared war on 29 July. Expected German help. Russia mobilised.

1914	Japan joins on side of Triple Entente (Allies) and Turkey on side of Triple Alliance. Defence of the realm Act (DORA) passed in Britain, bringing censorship, shutting pubs etc. – very unpopular!
1914	4 August: Britain declared war on Germany, because she had invaded Belgium to get to France quickly. BEF sent to Belgium.
1915	British and Empire forces attack Gallipoli. Major disaster. Italy enters war on the side of Britain and France.
1915	Trench warfare established in France. Soon became stalemate as neither side could break through the other's defences, largely due to effectiveness of machine guns. New weapons tried, without success, – e.g. aircraft, gas (first by Germans against Russians).
1915	Germans began submarine (U-boat) war in attempt to starve Britain of supplies and food. Rationing began in Germany.
1916	Germans try and fail to capture Verdun in effort to break stalemate in trenches. Similar attempt by British at River Somme also fails. Very heavy casualties in both cases. British even tried with small number of tanks.
1916	Naval battle off the Jutland peninsula between British and German fleets. No clear winner.
1916	Conscription started in Britain. Rationing in Britain. Convoy system introduced to defeat U-boat attacks. Food riots in Germany, many starved to death.
1917	America joins Allies because of German U-boat activities and German encouragement to Mexico to think of attacking Texas, Arizona.
1917	Russian revolution. Russia makes peace with Germany. Many German troops could now be moved to France.
1917	British tanks used successfully at battle of Cambrai. Trench stalemate seems broken.
1918	March: Major German attack all along front line forcing the Allies back in many places. Allies about to halt the advance and then counter-attack in August. October: German sailors mutinied at Kiel and unrest spread through Germany. November: all German allies had been forced to surrender and Germany was left to fight alone. Kaiser fled to Holland and abdicated. 11 November Germany accepted Allied terms for cease fire. War ended.
1919–20	Treaty of Versailles: set out harsh peace terms Germany had to accept. The Allies meant to punish Germany and make her weak. Many Germans hated the treaty. League of Nations was set up to protect world peace. America did not join and Germany was not allowed to join. League had no army and had to rely on persuasion or economic sanctions to keep peace.
1923	France invaded the Ruhr, a major German industrial area, because Germany had not paid reparations.
1926	Germany allowed to join League of Nations
1928	65 countries signed the Kellogg Pact agreeing not to resort to war to settle disputes.

Unit III

Glossary
GERMANY 1918–1939

Beer Hall Putsch   In 1923 Hitler attempted to start a revolution against the Weimar government by seizing power in Munich. His actions were poorly planned and failed but he was not punished severely and learned from his mistakes.

Concentration camps   Initially set up as prison camps run by the Brownshirts after Hitler came to power. Intended for anyone who opposed Nazi ideas. Later became part of the attempt to exterminate Jews.

Free Corps   (Freikorps) Troops who were disbanded at the end of the First World War but did not return to civilian life, remaining instead as brigades who were opposed to the peace terms, communists and many of the changes in Germany. They could be used by the government or by right wing opponents of it, like Wolfgang Kapp.

Fuhrer   Hitler took the title of 'Leader' (Fuhrer) when he became president of Germany in 1934. He then held absolute power and set out to establish a new German empire (Reich).

Gestapo   Secret State Police. Set up in 1933 and run by Heinrich Himmler from 1934, its task was to remove all enemies of the state and the extermination of the Jews. It acted as an instrument of terror above the law.

Goebbels, Joseph   1897–1945. Hitler's right hand man. Organiser of the Nazi propaganda machine from 1928.

Himmler, Heinrich   1900–1945. Took part in the Beer Hall Putsch and became head of the SS and later the Gestapo. Finally tried to betray Hitler in 1945.

Hitler Youth Organisations   for youngsters from the age of six. Separate organisations for boys and girls. Both encouraged to be loyal to Nazi ideals. Boys given games, uniforms etc. of a military nature. Girls encouraged to plan for motherhood and family life.

Hitler, Adolf   1889–1945. Born in Austria. Volunteered for German army in 1914 and was several times decorated during the war. Hated the peace settlement and believed in the superiority of Germans (Aryans) and was determined to restore German control in Europe. His Nazi party controlled Germany from 1933, using violence and propaganda. He built up German economic and military strength enormously 1933–1939.

Hyperinflation   When a government has to print massive quantities of paper money to try to pay its debts. Money becomes worthless and thousands were ruined. People had to live by barter.

Kapp Putsch   The attempt in 1920 by nationalist, Wolfgang Kapp, to seize power in Berlin using a Free Corps brigade. Members of the government fled the city because the regular army would not act against the Free Corps, but the workers went on strike and Kapp could not run the city or get the publicity he needed.

Master race   Nazis supported the belief that the Aryan race was superior to all others and used this to excuse attacks on inferior races such as the Jews or Czechs.

Nazi Party   Founded in 1919 by Anton Drexler but taken over by Hitler. Its main aims were set out in a programme of 25 points which included the destruction of the Treaty of Versailles, the restoration of Germany to her rightful place in Europe and purification of the German race.

Nuremberg Rallies   Propogananda for the Nazis in the form of mass meetings with the emphasis on ceremonial, uniforms, flags, rousing speeches.

Reparations   Germany was blamed for the First World War and as part of the peace terms had to agree to pay enormous sums of money to help her enemies recover. The huge amounts were also meant to cripple Germany and did lead to economic collapse in 1923.

SA and SS   The Brownshirts (SA) were the original supporters of the Nazi party, organised in disciplined gangs to terrorise its opponents. Hitler later created an elite personal guard and military force (SS) with black uniforms and fanatical devotion to himself and the Nazis.

Spartacists   Took their name from the Russian slave (Spartacus) who organised a revolution against the Roman empire. Tried to overthrow Ebert and the temporary government set up in Germany in 1918. Defeated later by the Free Corps in bitter street fighting in Berlin.

War Guilt   Germany was forced to accept that she alone was responsible for the First World War and all its costs in human life and suffering. Many Germans felt this was totally unfair and supported nationalists like Hitler who attacked this idea and the Treaty of Versailles who forced it on Germany.

Weimar Republic   Name used to describe the first elected government to take power and draw up a new constitution after the abdication of Kaiser Wilhelm II. Took its name from the small town of Weimar where it met because of unrest in Berlin.

Time Line
GERMANY 1918–1939

1918	Thousands die from outbreak of Spanish flu. In October German sailors mutiny at Kiel naval base. Riots and unrest all over Germany. Government feared revolution, as in Russia in 1917. In November crowds march on government buildings in Berlin. Kaiser forced to abdicate and flee to Holland. Republic set up under Friedrich Ebert. Agreed to harsh peace terms with Allies. In December Spartacist violence in Berlin.
1919	In January Spartacists renamed themselves the German Communist Party, and led by Rosa Luxemburg and Karl Leibknecht organised an uprising in Berlin. Ebert used the ex-soldiers of the Free Corps to defeat the uprising. Luxemburg and Leibknecht were murdered. Ebert confirmed as leader (President) of Germany and a new parliament (Reichstag) met in Weimar.
1919	In June final terms of peace settlement set out in Treaty of Versailles. Germany forced to accept blame for the war, pay enormous fines (reparations) to the allies and give up lands and its arms. Many Germans hated the treaty and the government for accepting it.
1920	Hitler founded the Nationalist Socialist German Workers Party (Nazis), the Kapp Putsch. Gustav Kapp tried to seize power in Berlin using Free Corps. Only failed because city workers went on strike, cutting off power, transport, water.
1921	First reparation payment due. Germany unable to pay all the money demanded by France and Belgium. Hitler set up the Brownshirts (SA) to attack opponents and force people to support him.
1923	France invaded the German industrial area of the Ruhr because reparations not paid. German government encourage people not to cooperate with the French troops. Germany facing severe money problems because of the rapid (hyper) inflation. Hitler tried to seize power and overthrow the Weimar Republic Munich (Bavaria) in the Beer Hall Putsch. Failed but won much publicity and some popular support.
1924	German economy began to recover with financial help from USA under the Dawes Plan and relaxation of reparation demands.
1925	Hitler refounded the Nazi party and set up the SS as an elite group within the Brownshirts. Local Nazi organisations set up Hitler Youth groups. First Nazi mass rally at Nuremberg.
1926	Germany allowed to join the League of Nations.
1928	Communists won four times as many seats as the Nazis in the German parliament.
1929	Wall Street Crash in the USA suddenly ended American investment in Germany causing economic collapse – businesses failed, unemployment rose steeply.

1930	Support for Nazi party growing because government seemed unable to cope. Nazis now second strongest party in parliament.
1932	Nazis became largest party in parliament in a violent election contest – 99 killed.
1933	Hitler became Chancellor, Reichstag (Parliament House) set on fire possibly by a communist. Hitler used this as an excuse to destroy the Communist party. Trade Unions also attacked. Hitler passed a law (the Enabling Act) giving the Nazis power for four years to control or destroy all who opposed them without asking for parliament's approval.
1933	Gestapo was founded. Concentration camps began. Suppression of Jews began. Nazi government signed Concordat (Agreement) with Catholic church to leave the church alone.
1934	Night of the Long Knives. Ernst Rohm and other leaders of the Brownshirts were arrested or killed because Hitler felt they were not fully loyal. Hitler became President as well as Chancellor when Hindenburg died. Called himself 'Der Fuhrer' (the leader) and now had absolute power in Germany.
1935	Nuremberg Race Laws passed – banning marriage between Jews and non-Jews.
1936	Hitler introduced Four Year Plan to restore German economy and build up her armed forces (secretly). National Labour Service used to provide employment in public works such as motorway building.
1936	Hitler sent troops into the Rhineland against the conditions of the Treaty of Versailles. Britain and France failed to take action against him. Germany made alliance with Italy and Japan.
1937	Nazis organised unrest in Austria to open the way for uniting Austria with Germany (Anschluss).
1938	Crystal Night. Nazi gangs attacked Jewish homes and businesses. Many Jews arrested. German troops moved into Austria. Shortly afterward Austrians 'voted' to unite with Germany.
1939	Germany invaded Czechoslovakia and then Poland causing the outbreak of the Second World War.

Glossary
RUSSIA 1914–1941

Autocracy   Form of government in which supreme power lies with one person – e.g. the Tsar.

Bolsheviks   Followers of Lenin. Revolutionaries who wanted to replace monarchy in Russia with a communist state.

Bourgeoisie   Middle class business people. Disliked by Communists because they owned property and wealth.

Capitalism   Ownership of businesses, factories and wealth by individuals.

CHEKA   Communist secret police set up in 1918. Later known as GPU or OGPU or NKVD.

Collectivisation   State ownership of all land. Peasants either worked as farm labourers for a wage on state farms (Sovkhoz) or on collective farms (Kolkhoz) where families worked for the state but were also allowed small pieces of land to work for themselves.

Comintern   An international organisation of communist parties set up in 1919.

Communism   The idea that all property and wealth belongs to all the people – that is, the state.

Five Year Plans   Stalin's attempts to modernise Russia by setting industry targets which had to be met. They had some success but less than was hoped for initially.

Kulaks   Peasants who had been successful since 1918. But 1918 almost all land was owned by peasants and Stalin wanted to change this. The most successful peasants were treated as enemies of the state and were attacked and their land was seized.

Lenin   1870–1924. Became a Marxist as a student. Mainly out of Russia between 1907 and 1917. Leader of the Bolshevik party. Allowed to return to Russia by the Germans because he wanted to end the war. Organised the overthrow of the Provisional Government in November 1917.

NEP   New Economic Policy. In 1921 Lenin allowed a partial return to private ownership and capitalism in Russia to help economic and social recovery after the civil war and to win back the support of the peasants.

Politburo   Set up in 1919 and became the ruling group within the Communist Party.

Provisional Government   The politicians who took over from the Tsar in 1917 as a temporary government until a new government could be elected.

Purges   1934–1938. Stalin attempted to destroy all his opponents by claiming there was a conspiracy to overthrow both him and Communist government. Suspects were arrested and faced rigged trials or were simply murdered by the secret police.

Rasputin   Corrupt 'holy man' who was close adviser to the Tsarina. Hated by Russian nobles and finally murdered by some of them.

Reds   Communist forces in the Russian civil war.

Stalin   1879–1953. Rose to power after the civil war but Lenin did not trust him. Opponent of Trotsky because of Trotsky's support for world communism. All-powerful in Russia in the 1930s.

Trotsky   Supporter of Lenin and organiser of the Red Guards who won the civil war for the Communists. Believed in spreading communist ideas from Russia to the rest of the world. Defeated and exiled by Stalin.

War Communism   Lenin's attempt to organise factories on military lines to increase output. Strikes were forbidden and middle class professionals brought in to run essential business. Peasants forced to give up food for the town workers.

Whites   Opponents of the Communists in the civil war. Some were monarchist, others republicans.

Time Line
RUSSIA 1914–1941

1914	In August Germany declared war on Russia.
1915	Russian armies heavily defeated by Germans. Tsar took command and went to the Front.
1916	Russian troops restless and unhappy because of poor leadership and lack of essential supplies. Rasputin assassinated by group of Russian nobles.
1917	In March riots in Petrograd because of food shortages and the war. Some soldiers mutinied and attacked government buildings. Tsar forced to abdicate. Monarchy abolished and a Provisional Government took over until elections could be held. Workers 'Soviets' (Councils) spread through the towns.
1917	In April Lenin returned to Russia from Switzerland. Attacked the Provisional Government in his 'April Theses'. Demanded 'Peace Bread Land'.
1917	July Days: serious unrest in Petrograd. Provisional Government blamed Lenin and the Bolsheviks and Lenin had to flee to Finland. In September the troops under General Kornilov marched on Petrograd to seize power. Stopped by Bolsheviks.
1917	In November Bolshevik Red Guards seized the Winter Palace and began a revolt against the Provisional Government which was facing major problems because of the war and major shortages. Bolsheviks gained control of only a small part of Russia.
1918	Constituent Assembly met to decide how Russia was to be governed. It was a mixture of Bolsheviks and Socialist Revolutionary party members.
1918	Russia made a humiliating peace with Germany, losing land and people.
1918	In April start of civil war in Russia between the Reds (Communists) and the Whites (monarchists, republicans). Whites controlled most of Russia and were supported by Britain, France and USA but were split over what they wanted. In July the Tsar and his family executed in Ekaterinburg by local branch of the CHEKA.
1918	War Communism set up by Lenin to give Communists right to control all land and resources.
1919	Communist winning civil war. Foreign powers began to withdraw after end of the First World War. International committee of Communist parties set up (Comintern).
1920	Polish invasion of Russia defeated. Reds won civil war.
1921	War Communism failing. Russia faced famine and economic collapse. In March strikes and unrest in Petrograd. Mutiny of sailors at Kronstadt naval base. Peasant uprisings against the Communists. Lenin announced the New Economic Policy (NEP) which allowed some private ownership and the use of money in Russia again.
1992	Lenin ill. Power struggle amongst those who wished to take over from him. Stalin and Trotsky were the main rivals.

1923	Union of Soviet Socialist Republics (USSR) created with Moscow as the capital of Russia.
1924	Lenin died having tried to make sure Stalin did not succeed him as party leader.
1925	Stalin forced Trotsky to give up position as Commissar for War. Communist Party accepted Stalin's view that Russia should concentrate on communism within USSR.
1927	Trotsky forced out of the Communist Party and exiled two years later.
1928	Stalin set up first Five Year Plan, to modernise major industries in Russia and increase output.
1929	Collectivisation of agriculture begun. Kulaks attacked.
1932	Second Five Year Plan – began early because of lack of success of first plan.
1934	Russia joined the League of Nations.
1934–38	Purges. Stalin organised a series of murders and show trials to 'purge' the Communist Party and the government of his enemies.
1936	Russia given a new and seemingly democratic constitution. In fact the promised rights were never granted and reforms were not made.
1937	Third Five Year Plan – interrupted by the race to build armaments for the Second World War.
1938	Trial of Bukharin and Rykov. By now Stalin had got rid of most of the original Bolshevik leaders.
1939	Russia made a non-aggression pact with Germany which allowed Germany to invade Poland, starting the Second World War.
1941	Germany invaded Russia.